How to Renovate Townhouses and Brownstones

How to Renovate Townhouses and Brownstones

William H. Edgerton

VNR VAN NOSTRAND REINHOLD COMPANY
NEW YORK   CINCINNATI   ATLANTA   DALLAS   SAN FRANCISCO
LONDON   TORONTO   MELBOURNE

Van Nostrand Reinhold Company Regional Offices:
New York   Cincinnati   Atlanta   Dallas   San Francisco

Van Nostrand Reinhold Company International Offices:
London   Toronto   Melbourne

Copyright © 1980 by Litton Educational Publishing, Inc.

Library of Congress Catalog Card Number: 79-24962
ISBN: 0-442-24841-5

All rights reserved. No part of this work covered by the copyright hereon may be reproduced or used in any form or by any means—graphic, electronic, or mechanical, including photocopying, recording, taping, or information storage and retrieval systems—without permission of the publisher.

Manufactured in the United States of America

Published by Van Nostrand Reinhold Company
135 West 50th Street, New York, N.Y. 10020

Published simultaneously in Canada by Van Nostrand Reinhold Ltd.

15 14 13 12 11 10 9 8 7 6 5 4 3 2 1

Library of Congress Cataloging in Publication Data

Edgerton, William H
   How to renovate townhouses and brownstones.

   Includes index.
   1. Row houses—Conservation and restoration.
I. Title.
NA 7520.E34   728.3'1   79-24962
ISBN 0-442-24841-5

Introduction

Satisfying an urge to renovate a row house can be frustrating, can consume endless amounts of time, patience and money, can threaten a marriage, alienate friends and employer, present unbelievable legal complications, and occasionally end in bankruptcy for the owner. However, all sorts of people, from newlyweds to grandparents, are charting such a rocky course for themselves in increasing numbers in many cities across the country. The obvious explanation lies in the challenge presented by a carefully conceived and well executed renovation and the financial rewards which are possible. The results invariably are satisfying, particularly in larger cities where in contrast to the concrete-steel-glass trilogy of commercial structures, the attractive, warm charm of the reconstructed row house stands as a lasting example of good residential accommodation.

While the old row house may retain its unique high ceilings, tall windows, working fireplaces, ample closet and storage areas, as well as adequate air and light both front and back, conveniences such as modern air conditioning, new baths, and up-to-date kitchens may be incorporated. These renovated buildings combine the best of both the nineteenth and the twentieth centuries.

Having become sufficiently intrigued to arrange for the purchase of a row house in its "native state" and having experienced all the complexities of renovating his building according to his own design, the average owner derives enough satisfaction and pleasure from the finished project, that he is apt to ask himself: "Why didn't I do this years ago?" and he often pictures himself in the guise of an authority on the subject of row house renovation! To be sure he is; however, only insofar as his own particular row house is concerned. These buildings vary, as people do, and each has a different heritage and a vastly different physical structure from all the others. As a consequence, renovating schemes for one type of building may not be entirely suitable to another, and no one can truly consider himself an "expert" in the complex field of row house renovation.

In addition to the personal satisfaction so important in row house renovation, there are other qualifications which are equally important. Few buildings are renovated for the sole occupancy of a single family; practically all such buildings, while providing living space for the owner, also include individual living units or apartments for rental purposes. These apartments may be confined to a single floor or may expand into two and three floors, according to the builder-owner's ideas. The fact that these apartments exist presupposes not only owner-occupancy and rental problems, but also the responsibility for maintenance and repair, so that row house renovation cannot be considered as reconstruction alone. Competent supervision and management must also be considered.

Little attempt will be made to discuss any management problems after completion, answers to which are readily available from other sources. The entire book will concentrate on questions such as:

1. How to find and choose the "right" building.
2. How to estimate purchase and renovation costs.
3. How to adequately finance the project.
4. How to select and work effectively with the professionals who will be responsible for carrying out the renovation.

From his own experience reconstructing two row houses, the author believes that there is an urgent need for a guide such as this to acquaint the newcomer to the field with many of the outstanding problems he will face and generally to encourage this particular form of urban living. Practically all of the larger metropolitan areas throughout the United States face the problem of rehabilitating tens of thousands of deteriorated dwellings. To help cities regain their former economic independence, such reconstruction plans are of critical importance, and row house renovation must be thought of as an integral part of this activity.

While the more specialized interests of the experienced individual will not be neglected, the primary objective of the book is to present valuable data and critical discussion pertinent to the field, and to suggest various renovation techniques for the benefit of the newcomer to row house renovation. The book contains an evaluation of the types of buildings on the market, the pros and cons of different renovation and rebuilding schemes, the predictable risks involved in each, the extent of personal participation and involvement, the necessary professional services to be used, and the varying amounts of capital required. Some of the material found in the introductory portions of the book, although extremely informative to everyone interested in row house problems, may relate to situations which may be already well known to the reader from personal experience.

The term row house is used throughout this book for convenience. The term can apply equally to townhouse, brownstone, limestone and attached dwelling.

For the sake of convenience "he" is used throughout the book in references to owner architect, etc. But of course the author is directing this book equally to women who are becoming the owners and renovators of row houses in ever-increasing numbers, as well as working in renovation-related jobs or professions.

Acknowledgments

No single book can do complete justice to the many-faceted subject of row house renovation. The techniques that are employed and the considerations involved vary as much as the buildings themselves differ from one to another. I wish to acknowledge the very helpful contributions of James L. Adler, William Asmann, Robert Caigan, Austin Haldenstein, F. Stacy Holmes II, Harvey Katz, David Nahon, Edward Schneider, Irving Schneider, Raynor Rogers, J. Parker Sondheimer, and L. McDonald Schetky, which have been invaluable in making *How to Renovate Townhouses and Brownstones* as complete and accurate as possible.

I also wish to thank the scores of persons who knowingly or unknowingly contributed comments, ideas, and efforts to the preparation of this book. In addition I must express a great debt to the men and women whose foresight over the last two centuries caused these buildings to be constructed, and to the individuals and families of our cities who have undertaken renovation projects in sufficient quantities and with enough questions to indicate a need for a work such as this. And, of course, for generous and intelligent help and understanding from start to finish, my wife, Ann, deserves the most grateful credit line of all.

WILLIAM H. EDGERTON

Contents

Introduction / v
1 General Categories of Row House Renovation / 1
2 Row House Location and Neighborhood Analysis / 13
3 Negotiating Strategy in Purchasing a Row House / 19
4 Condominiums, Cooperatives, and Partnerships / 23
5 Management Prior to Renovation / 29
6 Relocation of Tenants / 36
7 Insurance: Prior to and During Construction / 41
8 Legal Aspects of Row House Renovation / 47
9 The Architect / 55
10 The Architect's Role / 61
11 Row House Interior Design / 71
12 Row House Financing / 77
13 Standard Row House Existing Construction / 84
14 The Contractor / 87
15 Building Costs / 94
16 Security / 102
17 Telephone Installation and Service / 112
18 General Operation After Renovation / 114
19 Owner-Tenant Relations / 116
20 Personal Property Insurance After Construction / 120
Appendix 1 Check List of Forms or Documents Which May Be Required in Row House Renovation / 123
Appendix 2 Standard Form of Agreement Between Owner and Architect / 125
Appendix 3 Standard Form of Agreement Between Owner and Contractor / 139
Index / 147

Chapter 1
General Categories of Row House Renovation

More row house renovations fail due to inadequate research, planning, or financial analyses than for any other reason, and before making any decisions regarding the purchase of a row house the prospective buyer must have the answers to the following questions and problems.

APPROXIMATE AMOUNTS OF CASH REQUIRED FOR:

1. Purchase
2. Renovation
3. Professional and technical services

NATURE AND SCOPE OF RENOVATION:

1. Retention or demolition of major parts of the structure
2. Installation of new elements or systems
3. Rearrangement of individual floor plans
4. Decision relative to single-floor or multiple-floor living units

APPROXIMATE AMOUNT OF TIME REQUIRED FOR:

1. Purchase of building
2. Financing
3. Demolition
4. Reconstruction
5. Finishing

SERVICES AND FEES OF SPECIALISTS, SUCH AS:

1. Real estate broker
2. Attorney
3. Architect
4. Contractor

MISCELLANEOUS, RELATED ITEMS, SUCH AS:

1. Location of row house
2. Relation to adjacent buildings
3. Caliber of the neighborhood
4. Tenants involved
5. External structural features
6. Dimensions of property
7. Extent of free ground (yards), if any

With these facts and figures in his possession, the prospective buyer can then tailor his purchase to his bank balance, alert to all sorts of potential problems and complications which could arise, and ultimately occupy the type of row house which will not only satisfy his personal living needs, but also afford him a reliable source of continuing income in the form of rents.

Contractors who are familiar with row houses and their related renovation problems usually distinguish between six or seven specific types. The list ranges from a building completely renovated by professionals and requiring little or no further alteration, to a structure which is in such a state of deterioration and disrepair that only the exterior walls and interior structure such as subfloors and beams are worth saving.

While the building renovated by professionals demands extensive capital as an initial investment, no personal demands are made upon the prospective buyer, as all reconstruction has been completed. Furthermore, there is no guesswork as to the outcome of the construction process; the investor sees what he is buying and he can usually obtain a long-term financing commitment from a bank with a minimum of delay. In direct contrast, the individual who decides on a much lower priced row house for instance, one which must be "gutted" before any renovation can begin embarks on an unpredictable adventure of his own making. To be sure, for the latter, the capital investment may be less, but the risks are that much greater. There can never be any guarantee that plans, however detailed, will materialize in three dimensions as originally drawn, and costs always seem to exceed estimates. However, the results are extremely personal and can therefore be unique.

From this brief comparison it is obvious that there are several different approaches to row house renovation, and that there are many complex professional and technical features to be carefully considered. The type of building chosen for renovation is a critical choice, and the reader will be better oriented if he first considers various detailed row house renovation ideas according to three general categories which present generalizations that will be covered more fully in subsequent chapters:

1. Large-scale reconstruction
2. Modified renovation
3. Renovation completed prior to purchase

The prospective row house owner must see through the paint and grime of an unrestored building and see the basic structure beneath. With sound planning this building can be elegant once again.

All purchase prices quoted in the text pertain to the major portion of row houses available in New York City in the mid-1970's. Buildings in other areas may often be purchased at lower prices.

LARGE-SCALE RECONSTRUCTION

Prior to purchase, buildings found in this group usually were operated as rooming houses; some may be in comparatively good condition, but the majority are in extremely poor condition. In both instances large-scale reconstruction is mandatory.

General Features

1. Entire demolition of interior, leaving only the building "shell," or partial demolition, floor-by-floor, leaving the basic interior intact.
2. Professional services of attorney, banker, architect, contractor, technicians, etc., are required.
3. There is a considerable time-lag between actual purchase and occupancy.

Purchase Price Range

1. Total purchase price of the building: $60,000 - $120,000. (In some sections of some cities, however, row houses can be purchased for as low as $20,000 or even less, and, of course, in the very desirable areas premium prices are encountered.)
2. Immediately available capital necessary for purchase: $20,000 - $40,000.

Extent of Renovation

Interior demolition (partial or complete) and reconstruction.

Renovation Costs

Required (minimum quality levels): $60,000 - $100,000.

Time Required

1. Purchase: 3 months.
2. Preparatory planning (e.g. blueprints, financing arrangements, etc.): 3-9 months.
3. Relocation of tenants: 3-? months.
4. Demolition: 1-2 months.
5. Construction: 4-8 months.

Individuals Involved

1. Owner: not absolutely obligatory, but in the majority of instances, partial or extensive participation is recommended; in some few cases participation is mandatory.
2. Others: banker, attorney, architect, contractor are minimum.

Favorable Factors To Be Considered

1. Condition of building: when the interior of the row house has been demolished and entirely reconstructed, the investor becomes the owner of an essentially brand-new building. There is no necessity to compromise with any electrical, plumbing, heating, carpentry, or masonry half-measures; all installations are new. Furthermore, the completely renovated interior is structured according to the needs and taste of the owner. He ultimately comes into possession of his own house and at no time is he forced to accept any layout or architectural features which do not please him, with the only exception being one of features limited by their cost.
2. Price vs. income: the purchase price of this type row house is generally less than any other equivalent building, and with carefully drawn plans which are well-extended, the building should show a paper profit even during the first year of occupancy, provided 70% or more of the building is allocated to rentable apartments.
3. Owner's participation: renovation costs and satisfying results vary directly according to the extent of personal involvement on the part of the owner. If he maintains a constant and close association with his architect and builder, there will be opportunities to cut corners, not only in expenditures, but also in the time required for the project. The most effective way in which an owner may consider such an undertaking is as if he had accepted a second vocation. The more time the owner devotes to his renovation project, the better the outcome. And there is another way in which money may be saved. Where owners are experienced and capable of handling certain jobs themselves, such as refinishing existing woodwork which is to be retained, constructing shelving, etc., there is no need to pay the contractor for this work.
4. Building availability, income: once the renovation has been completed, there is nothing to prevent immediate occupancy. There are no existing tenant problems to complicate the situation. Having carefully planned the style of apartments he considers most attractive to tenants in that particular locality, either all efficiency units or a combination of efficiencies and larger apartments, rentals are immediate, for there is a large demand for well-planned apartments throughout the country.

6 HOW TO RENOVATE TOWNHOUSES AND BROWNSTONES

Adverse Factors To Be Considered

1. Renovation costs: while the actual purchase price of this type of row house usually requires a smaller initial capital investment than any other, renovation costs are that much higher. This emphasizes the necessity for extremely careful estimates and constant control and supervision on the part of the owner, for the financial benefit based on a low purchase price can be dissipated by uncontrolled construction costs (especially "extras").
2. Owner participation: the closer the association between the owner and his technical advisors, the less needless waste of money. New owners frequently show great personal enthusiasn at the start of such projects because of their novelty, and then often lose interest as the construction drags on. This may prove fatal to the individual's investment, for no hired person can be expected to watch the flow of cash as carefully as the one who is responsible for providing the funds.
3. Time required: constant delays will be encountered for any number of reasons, and unexpected complications will seem to multiply to the complete exasperation of the owner. These certainly will occur in spite of the most careful planning. As a consequence, no definite completion date can be depended upon in advance. An individual not temperamentally equipped to cope with such situations should shun all such renovation undertakings and purchase a completed building.

MODIFIED ROW HOUSE RENOVATION

This group consists of buildings that, sometime in the past, have already been converted into "self-contained" apartments, each unit provided with its own bathroom and kitchen facilities. However, for maximum return on the investment (higher rentals), extensive renovation is necessary.

General Features

1. This group covers buildings already divided into self-contained living units, and buildings which retain their original room-by-room layout either ex-rooming houses or one-family dwellings.
2. These buildings, generally, are in good structural condition, however, paint, plaster and trim vary from average to bad.
3. In instances where apartments and/or rooms exist and are occupied prior to purchase, there are tenant relocation problems.
4. There may be a considerable time-lag between purchase and availability for occupancy.
5. Professional services of an attorney, banker, architect, contractor, technicians, etc., are required. A comparison of alternate building types appears on the following page.

GENERAL CATEGORIES OF ROW HOUSE RENOVATION

Figure 1. Row house comparison chart.*

	ROW HOUSES WITH APARTMENTS		ROW HOUSES WITHOUT APARTMENTS			
			ROOMING HOUSES		ONE-FAMILY HOUSES	
Purchase price range	$60,000–$200,000		$40,000–$150,000		$70,000–$200,000	
Capital required	$25,000–$ 40,000		$15,000–$ 25,000		$50,000–$ 60,000	
Type of renovation	Moderate	Minimal	Returned to single family status	Apartments created	Single family status retained	Apartments created
Renovation costs	$40,000–$120,000	$20,000–$80,000	$10,000–$50,000	$25,000–$120,000	$5,000–$80,000	$25,000–$120,000
Time required for renovation	9–24 months	9–24 months	3–8 months	6–18 months	2–6 months	6–18 months

*Depends on the city, and area within the city. Use as a rough guide only.

Individuals Involved

1. Owner: participation of the owner is optional; however, the closer the association between the owner and those undertaking the renovation, the more time and money saved.
2. Others: banker, attorney, architect, contractor, and other technicians are required. Existing row houses without apartments, converted to single-family occupancy, can be handled with minimal professional assistance, or on a do-it-yourself basis both with significant savings in cost.

Factors to Consider

1. General condition of building: as far as the interior structure is concerned, row houses in this group are usually in rather good condition. The never-converted, one-family house is often in outstanding condition, and the rooming house may be considered the worst of the lot on the basis of deteriorated surfaces, finishes, and mechanical systems. Although buildings which have already been divided into apartments may require nominal alterations to suit the owner, the major renovation has already been attended to. It is a question of alteration, rather than rebuilding except in situations where a duplex or a triplex apartment is desired.

    The never-converted one-family, and the rooming houses offer the greatest latitude in type of renovation, since both are in their original state. Reconstruction can be planned according to the purchaser's taste and pocketbook. Other buildings, subdivided into individual apartments at the time of purchase, present a definite challenge, should major rather than minor changes be contemplated. Such changes call for careful planning to avoid incurring additional and often unnecessary costs.
2. Purchase price vs. income: row houses with apartments offer a practical and financial compromise to the buyer. He may move into one, and still continue to rent one or more of the others, even during remodeling. (Occupancy is usually not allowed during major reconstruction.) In addition, this particular class of renovation may be undertaken at a pace and cost convenient to the owner.

    These row houses, however, are no particular "bargains," and the buyer must expect to spend more in reconstruction dollars for a rooming house where major reconstruction is in order, than on a building which already has been divided into apartments.
3. Extent of renovation: the never-converted single-family and rooming houses require the most extensive reconstruction, since they must be considered as being in their original state at the time of

purchase. There is one advantage of the single-family house, that of its being occupied at once, provided the buyer is content to accept conditions as they are, while rooming houses, mainly because of the previous type of occupancy, have no such possibility.

Buildings which contain apartments, rent-controlled or decontrolled, may require only minor remodeling, provided the new owner is satisfied with what has been done to the building.

4. Time and capital required for reconstruction: any remodeling, or changes in floor plans of row houses divided into apartments, may be undertaken at the discretion of the owner. Arrangements can be made for a minimum of interruption to normal living conditions within the building, and can be tailored to funds currently available to the owner. The renovation of rooming houses, as a rule, is carried out at one time, during which the entire building is unavailable for occupancy. This situation dictates that the owner live elsewhere and have in his possession the requisite capital for the entire job. Construction often takes 12 or more months from the purchase date.

5. Owner participation and involvement: in row houses converted into apartments, where the owner occupies one of the units, he is readily available, particularly at the beginning and end of each day should the need for consultation arise. Close contact and personal supervision usually afford the owner the chance to not only save dollars, but also enable him to make "on-the-spot" decisions. In instances where certain changes are comparatively minor, an owner may undertake them himself, thereby saving money.

6. Personal satisfaction: the only too often dirty, squalid rooming house provides the new owner with as much latitude of expression, surprisingly, as does the pristine "jewel" of a one-family house which has always been well cared for by its occupants. Basically, both of these buildings may demand major renovation. As a consequence, the buyer finds himself in the position of being able to express unlimited choice, and plans may be extremely personalized. In such instances, where renovation costs are of secondary concern, unusual floor layouts may be introduced. While such features enhance rentals, and even the value of the entire property, the larger investment usually causes the buyer to settle for an arrangement of conventional apartments, one or two to a floor.

RENOVATION COMPLETED PRIOR TO PURCHASE

Cooperatives and condominiums are included in this group although they are discussed separately in Chapter 4.

General Features

1. Minor, or no renovation required.
2. Minor, or no tenant problems.
3. Apartment units not covered by rent control.
4. Rental income assured from date of purchase.

Purchase Price Range

1. Total cost of row house: $110,000–$250,000, with some buildings in very desirable sections priced up to $500,000.
2. Immediately available capital required: $35,000–$110,000 (depending upon financing).

Extent of Renovations

1. Required: none.
2. Optional: nominal (such as kitchens, appliances, etc.).

Renovation Costs

1. Required: none.
2. Optional: nominal (small amount in relation to purchase price).

Time Required

Since any and all alterations are necessarily minor, the time element cannot be considered an important factor.

Individuals Involved

1. Owner: provided the alterations are relatively minor, and the owner is sufficiently interested and able, all such work probably can be completed without assistance from anyone other than a contractor.
2. Others: should the owner not be interested and/or incapable of undertaking the minor alterations, outside individuals must be engaged to plan and complete the work.

Favorable Factors To Be Considered

1. Condition of building: with all major reconstruction completed the buyer purchases what he can see. He either likes or dislikes what has been done to the building.
2. Purchase price: the investor must have the necessary cash to swing the purchase with or without a mortgage. The purchase price is fixed or negotiated to a fixed amount: there are no additional hidden or unforeseen expenditures involved except when the buyer wishes to make some minor alterations after purchase.

Row house conversions can be so complete that nothing is left of the original building. Note the garage door, evidence of a luxury incorporated in very few row houses.

3. Personal involvement of owner: ordinary renovation problems have already been experienced by the developer who planned and executed the reconstruction. The buyer's only involvement is moving into his newly acquired living quarters, and renting those apartments which were not previously rented.
4. Availability income: following his purchase, the new owner may take immediate occupancy, and since he is able to rent the other apartments in the building at the same time, his income from the building may be considered as commencing on the day of title transfer.

Adverse Factors To Be Considered

1. Purchase price vs. profit: since the prior owner had invested his own money and assumed the burden and responsibility of renovation, he must be properly compensated for the risks taken and the labor involved. The prospective buyer must realize that he is not only paying for reconstruction expenses and professional fees, but in his purchase price he is also providing a reasonable margin of profit to the builder or developer.

   As one might expect, the purchase price of an already renovated row house is high. Normally, it will exceed any and all expenditures made by a prospective owner who selects and contracts with his own group of specialists and supervises the progress of the reconstruction. Ascending real estate prices will usually afford an equitable profit to the owner who ultimately wishes to sell his property, but since his purchase price was high, his percentage of profit will be less.
2. Alteration feasibility: during construction when the owner works closely with the architect or contractor, minor practical and/or desirable changes in construction may be made on the spot, with little extra cost or loss of time. In contrast, once the construction has been completed, the same type of change may entail considerable additional expense and great inconvenience, often to the entire building. Changes which might have been feasible during the reconstruction may later prove impractical or too costly.
3. Personal satisfaction: how does one compare the personal satisfaction of watching one's own renovation plans materialize, with that of buying a renovated row house which embodies someone else's ideas? In actuality, the former expresses the owner's personality. Writing a check for a building entirely remodeled by others is immeasurably easier but not as satisfying as planning ones own renovation.

   It is entirely up to the prospective investor to decide whether he wishes to saddle himself with work, sweat, frustration, and ultimately end with a building renovated to suit his tastes, or bypass all these unpleasantries and accept the work of others at a higher price.

Chapter 2
Row House Location and Neighborhood Analysis

An old saying reminds us that the three most important factors concerning a parcel of real estate are location, location, and location. They are equally important in the choice of a particular row house. No building should be purchased without careful scrutiny of both the immediate block and the surrounding neighborhood.

If possible, the prospective owner should obtain reliable information regarding adjacent buildings as well as those on the opposite side of the street. This information should include.

1. How many have purchased within the past 6 months? The past year? How do the purchase prices compare? Are they up, level, or down?
2. Are the houses well maintained? Have they been well renovated? Do the owners occupy the buildings?
3. How many buildings are completely rented? What is the caliber of the tenants? Are they law-abiding and quiet?
4. Are the front sidewalk portions of the buildings clean and neat? Is refuse collected regularly?

Information about the neighborhood itself is also of great importance. The prospective buyer should be interested in learning:

1. How much traffic passes on the street during the day? The night? Are there any congestion problems? What parking problems are there?
2. How much pedestrian traffic is there? Does there seem to be any latent problem concerning undesirable groups, loiterers?
3. Is there reasonable police protection day and/or night? Is there a Fire Department alarm box within a reasonable distance? How many fire hydrants are there nearby?
4. What about adequate street lighting?
5. Does any block association exist? What are its dimensions? How effective are its activities?

The location should also be considered from the point of view of facilities offered, such as:

1. What types of transportation are available? Is the location convenient to reaching main centers of the city?
2. Are schools in the vicinity? Are there any private schools available, should public schools be unacceptable?
3. Is shopping convenient? How do prices compare with other neighborhoods? How is the quality of the food? The variety, choice?
4. Are there any parks or recreational facilities nearby?
5. What are the distances to cultural activities, clubs, motion picture theaters? Which denominations are represented by churches in the neighborhood?

Factors influencing the real estate values of nearby buildings are of utmost importance, considering the high purchase price of most row houses and the cost of renovation. Pertinent information should be collected with regard to:

1. How does the owner's building compare in price with others on the block? Is it lower or higher in price?
2. Are real estate price levels for the block rising or declining?
3. Have the majority of the row houses been renovated? To what degree? What further renovation plans are contemplated?
4. What percentage of buildings are occupied by single families? How many consist of one-floor apartments? How many have duplexes? Triplexes?
5. Has there been excessive real estate speculation in the neighborhood? How many buildings have been sold immediately following renovation?

It is apparent from such a detailed list that certain prospective buyers will consider some items more important than others. However, it is recommended that such a careful survey be made of the neighborhood, if for no other reason than to acquaint the buyer with what he may expect after purchase. And the results of this survey should be discussed with other family members, an attorney, or other professional advisers to see if specific conclusions can be drawn from the answers.

Although armed with the above checklist, the prospective buyer can hardly expect to find a suitable building by merely covering neighborhood after neighborhood on foot, and inquiring every time he discovers a promising possibility. If this method does bring results, it must be ascribed to good fortune, not good planning. How, then, *does* one actually locate a row house which fits one's need? There are several sources to consult and methods to follow:

These six-story walk-up buildings cast substantial shadows on the adjoining row houses and affect the scale of a row house neighborhood.

Classified advertisements in the principal newspaper, particularly the real estate section of the Sunday issue, are usually the single most valuable source.

Neighborhood publications often carry current offerings of row houses which frequently turn out to be extremely important leads since the cost of advertising in such publications is lower than in the principal papers, which appeals to row house sellers. However, the listings are sometimes limited and frequently inaccurate. Friends who own row houses are very good sources for locating available buildings. Although buyers of apartments rarely go out of their way to influence their friends to follow suit, in contrast, the row house owner automatically becomes a member of a "movement"; he enjoys discussing his renovation schemes and accomplishments with others. As might be expected, friends who own or have rehabilitated their homes frequently are able to provide clues to other excellent possibilities in their neighborhood and they probably are the single best source of information and guidance. Additionally, there is no better way to become personally acquainted with rehabilitation; friends have nothing to sell—except their enthusiasm—and the prospect is in a position to evaluate impartially.

Obviously a valuable source in locating a row house is a knowlegeable real estate broker who serves as an intermediary between the buyer and seller. After selecting such an agent, the usual procedure is to meet with him in his office. There, the prospective buyer can state his preferences as to building location, size, condition, etc., and the amount of capital he wishes to invest in the project. Establishing a sound working relationship in this manner, and acquainting the broker with personal preferences will save much valuable time, visiting unacceptable buildings or neighborhoods, since the broker has access to many listings of available buildings.

Real estate brokers are usually licensed by their state Department of Real Estate and in addition, the majority are members of the real estate board of their city. The state license is usually prominently displayed. Brokers often employ licensed salesmen to assist them in customer relations, securing listings, and in negotiating sales. There should be no hesitancy in dealing with these persons since the salesman may have more available time than the broker himself and thus prove to be of more real help.

The association with one's real estate broker should be just as businesslike as with any agent. The prospective buyer is often uninformed and wishes to obtain guidance and information; the broker is the most appropriate individual to provide this service. If there is mutual trust and confidence, results should be satisfying and a building purchased. It may not be possible, however, to create a completely satisfactory relationship with the first broker due to conflicting personalities or other reasons, and there may be a necessity to speak with several to find a satisfactory one.

The owner of a building that is for sale pays the brokerage fee; the buyer is not obliged to pay anyone anything, but in fact he ultimately agrees to a sales price that includes a commission. As a result of this financial arrangement the broker's first allegiance belongs to the seller from whom he receives his commission but this should not affect the relationship of the parties, all of whom are necessary for a satisfactory transaction.

It is not entirely uncommon for a broker to find that the prospective buyer is uninformed as far as row houses are concerned, and quite unfamiliar with problems associated with their renovation. The buyer can hardly expect the broker to supply all this missing knowledge, since, if he did so, there would be little time for his normal business. However, there is a standard practice by which the basics of row house renovation may be learned, and that is by engaging a broker, or someone equally well informed, as a consultant at a stipulated fee. In this way the consultant is compensated for his time, and the buyer can expect valid and unbiased answers to all his questions. For the uninitiated this arrangement works extremely well. There are also renovation courses held in many cities, for a modest fee.

Some buyers believe that there is a better chance of locating the row house that exactly fits their requirements when they "register" with several brokers; other buyers are content with no more than one or at the most two. The first method assures the buyer wide coverage of the field, while those who restrict themselves to only one or two brokers rely more upon close buyer-broker rapport to produce quicker and more satisfying results.

The real estate broker, like any other professional, varies according to native ability and personality. However, as a client, the buyer has the right to expect from his broker valid and precise information such as follows:

1. Frequent listings of available row houses accompanied by all pertinent data.
2. A statement regarding the positive and negative structural and finish features of these buildings.
3. A guide to general renovation cost for each.
4. The probable relation of an actual purchase price to the asking price.
5. Approximate annual operating costs and taxes.
6. Positive and negative aspects of the neighborhood.
7. A report on other recent sales in the immediate area.

In a completely satisfactory buyer-broker relationship some of the responsibilities must be reciprocal:

1. Buyer and One Broker
   a. When either personal interests or requirements regarding row houses change, the broker should be notified, thereby saving his time and effort.
   b. When purchase plans are vague, and the buyer is primarily interested in "window shopping," the broker should be so informed. A frank statement of this sort can in no way alienate the broker,

and will at the same time insure the buyer's name being retained on the broker's mailing list, should he so desire.

c. After having inspected several buildings, the buyer is obligated to personally convey his impressions to the broker.

d. The buyer should not expect to inconvenience all parties by demanding to see the same building over and over again, prior to a formal offer. Two visits should be sufficient, if there is actual interest, with a third in the company of an architect and/or contractor.

e. Ridiculously low bids should be avoided since they can lead to nothing more than antagonizing the seller. The broker should be able to state his opinion of what a reasonable offer might be, should the buyer be seriously interested.

f. After having found the row house which seems to meet all of his requirements, the buyer should not delay too long without valid cause. If he does not act swiftly he may lose the opportunity and the broker will have wasted needless time and effort.

g. Should a prospective buyer happen to learn the name of the owner of a building appearing on a broker's listing, he has no reason to ask that the owner show the premises, and certainly no justification in negotiating its purchase other than through the broker's office, since he will probably pay a price that includes a brokerage commission, if he ultimately buys. An exception would be his response to advertising asking for "principals only."

2. Buyer and Several Brokers

   a. To obtain the best results and to be fair, the buyer should make no attempt to hide the fact that he is working through more than one agent. When each broker is aware of this fact, there can be no possibility of conflict or misunderstanding.

   b. When a buyer has seen a certain building, each of the other brokers should be notified so the buyer may avoid being asked to visit the same location more than once.

   c. It is the buyer's obligation to maintain a list of houses he has seen, indicating when visited and by whom shown. Should there be an ultimate purchase of one of the buildings, a commission is usually payable to the broker who actually showed the building first.

   d. The buyer is obligated not to reveal listings of one broker to another.

   e. As a final suggestion to the buyer, should he happen to learn of a row house for sale and not be personally interested, it is a courtesy to inform the brokers he has worked with of this fact. This type of reciprocity never fails to bring returns, because listings of buildings for sale are a broker's stock-in-trade.

Chapter 3
Negotiating Strategy in Purchasing a Row House

When a prospective buyer finds a building to his liking, he must obtain all pertinent financial information. This is often supplied by the real estate broker's listing, but there may be discrepancies, and it is advisable that the buyer consult with a lawyer.

Most lawyers maintain that it is not their obligation to offer advice or make decisions relative to personal or financial matters for their clients, but the lawyer's role is an important one in a row house purchase. The lawyer becomes the buyer's legal protector during the purchasing maneuvers, offering legal advice, suggesting legal action, preparing necessary forms, and outlining mortgage provisions, purchase terms, etc. In these matters he is usually in a prime position to offer financial advice as well.

If any doubts about the reasonableness of the asking price persist after consulting with a lawyer, a real estate appraiser should be engaged. Although a real estate broker might be able to value the property, of these two, the appraiser must be considered the most objective observer for he has no stake in the transaction; he will receive between $150-$200 for his written valuation report. While the real estate broker can be expected to provide the buyer with guidelines to valid property values other factors are involved and his estimate may not prove to be impartial.

The property purchase prices which appear on real estate brokers' listings should be considered by the buyer as reliable. The buyer should act accordingly, and offering prices should not approach unrealistic limits. At this point the broker's advice is extremely valuable. Remember that the price, as well as the terms, found in the listing are probably negotiable to some extent. If a price is listed as "firm," it usually indicates that the price is *not* negotiable; however, some of the terms may be. Purchasers often place undue emphasis on purchase price, without sufficient regard for terms (i.e. length of purchase contract, size and interest rate of the mortgage, etc.) and these favorable terms may permit a prospective buyer to consider certain buildings which at first appear to be beyond his budget. Purchase price and terms should be discussed in detail with both the lawyer and the real estate broker. No offer should be made until the broker has ascertained whether any previous offers have been made to and rejected by the seller, thus fixing a level at which the seller refuses to act.

BROKER'S ROLE IN NEGOTIATING AN OFFER

When an offering price has been decided, it is the broker's obligation to present it to the seller. At the same time he may suggest to the seller that the building be taken off the market for a few days while negotiations are being conducted. If this request is refused, then the broker must keep the prospective buyer informed of any and all offers made by other individuals for the same property. As a note of warning at this juncture, the prospective buyer is urged to shun all suggestions of becoming involved in an "auction" with other buyers. Should an auction prove unavoidable, and the buyer be that much interested in a particular building, the most effective action is immediate purchase at whatever price is being asked.

BUYER-SELLER RELATIONS

The buyer's first offer invariably proves to be unacceptable to the seller; either purchase price or terms, or both, may prove to be stumbling blocks. Before making another offer, the buyer should find out as accurately as possible what amount the seller expects to receive. If the difference between the buyer's revised offer and the seller's demands is small intelligent negotiations should result in agreement within a few days. During this period the broker serves as an intermediary, keeping both parties constantly informed as to the progress of the negotiations. It is also advisable that the buyer maintain close contact with his lawyer for advice. Nothing is more exasperating to a lawyer than to be forced to renegotiate unfavorable terms which an uninformed buyer has previously agreed to accept.

When negotiations have reached a stalemate (as they frequently do), and there is wide divergence between offering and acceptance price, the buyer should propose a "final offer." If this, too, is rejected, then any and all offers should be withdrawn. However, the wise buyer may suggest that the broker keep him advised as to future availability of the property, should he wish to make a subsequent offer at some later date. Sellers have been known to revise their prices downward if no acceptable offers are forthcoming during a reasonable period.

There are times when tangled negotiations can be resolved by a buyer-seller conference which has been arranged and is attended by the broker. If advisable, the two lawyers may be invited to join the conference. Often situations which have arisen because of third-party intervention, or have become confused due to the lack of personal contact, disappear when both parties meet face-to-face. At such meetings the broker again acts as an

NEGOTIATING STRATEGY IN PURCHASING A ROW HOUSE 21

The planting of mature trees can enhance the value of a row house well beyond their cost. Window boxes often improve the appearance of a building when used on the first floor and provide a nice vista for the tenant within.

intermediary. Since he is well acquainted with the demands and the reasoning of both buyer and seller, he is in a position to suggest means of compromise. For instance, the cash position may be of utmost importance to the seller, while the mortgage terms may prove to be an obstacle to the buyer. Knowing both positions, the broker is able to propose solutions acceptable to both.

Once there is final agreement as to purchase price and terms, the lawyers confer to consider the technical aspects of the agreement. When final agreement is reached, the lawyers designate the time and date for preparing and signing the contract of sale. The purchaser then meets with his lawyer to discuss his obligations. At this time he learns when further action is required, and the details of the closing where, when, and how much money he is to make available.

Chapter 4
Condominiums, Cooperatives, and Partnerships

Two or more unrelated individuals owning and occupying a single piece of property is one way to proceed with a row house renovation project and this joint action can take the form of condominium, cooperative, or partnership ownership. Purchase prices and construction costs have been climbing so fast in recent years that cash requirements for the successful completion of a row house purchase and renovation have risen beyond the means of the average single investor. There still are some neighborhoods where row house renovations are relatively unique, or even unknown. There, the small number of reconstructions has not focused speculative attention, and price levels have not increased as fast as in other areas. In such areas it may still be possible to complete a five- or ten-unit building for a low investment of $20-30,000 cash. However, even this sum, when contrasted with the $40-50,000 in cash that may be required for the average project, may be beyond the reach of a prospective buyer. As a consequence, he is forced to consider other ways to handle the project.

CONDOMINIUMS

The condominium form of real estate ownership permits an individual or family to purchase a three-dimensional special unit (usually an apartment) together with an undivided share of the building's common elements such as hallways, basement, lobbies, elevators (if any), grounds, etc. Under this form of ownership, purchases and sales of apartments can be made either free and clear, or subject to mortgages as large or as small as the financial resources of the purchaser permit. The condominium purchaser receives a recordable deed indicating ownership of his dwelling unit exactly as he would were he buying a house. He may sell, rent, exchange, or mortgage his unit independent of actions taken by, or the wishes of, his neighbors. He also may deduct real estate taxes and mortgage interest on his federal income tax return in a manner identical to that of an owner of a single-family, detached house. The only difference is that in addition to his own maintenance costs, he also will have to pay his share of the maintenance and operating costs of the building's common areas, as indicated in the Master Lease or Declaration of Condominium Ownership.

Although this form of ownership appears to be suitable for row houses, condominium ownership does not provide any individual control of apartment resale. In many cities this factor seems to be of primary importance, particularly in small buildings where neighbor relations are sensitive at all times. Equally as important, condominium mortgages are difficult to obtain. A bank's legal work and mortgage servicing become much more involved when the number of units is large, and the dollars represented by each mortgage are small. Particularly in times of tight mortgage money, lenders are apt to prefer the simplicity of one large mortgage rather than several small ones. Moreover, in the event of nonpayment, the bank would be forced to initiate foreclosure proceedings against the individual owner, an action that is almost completely unknown in other forms of joint ownership.

Condominium ownership does dictate a much lower cash investment on the part of the owner-occupant, and this may be the explanation of why the arrangement has not been abandoned entirely in northern cities where lenders are less sympathetic to this form of ownership than states like Florida where it has been accepted for some time.

COOPERATIVES

In the cooperative form of real estate ownership of a row house, title to the building is held by a corporation. The owner buys stock representing ownership in the corporation, and executes and receives a proprietary lease from the corporation that entitles him to occupy his apartment unit. Each of the cooperative shareholders agrees to pay monthly carrying charges to cover his proportionate share of taxes, interest, and principal on the building's mortgage, insurance, maintenance, and other costs. The owner of a cooperative may sell and assign his stock and lease to another purchaser approved by the board of directors of the owning corporation, and he may sublet his apartment with similar approval.

The cooperative corporation, not the individual stockholder, has the legal responsibility for making payments under the terms of the building's mortgage. However, the corporation must depend upon its stockholders for prorata shares of such payments. In large cooperatives where there are over 50 apartments, if one owner defaults (i.e. becomes bankrupt, dies intestate, disappears, etc.), the other members of the cooperative corporation must apportion the missing funds among themselves, but the effect is minimal considering the number of remaining shareholders.

Row house cooperatives offer no such safety in numbers. If one owner in a 4-, 5-, or even 10-unit building defaults, the increased financial demand on the others is substantial. But the probability of this happening is lessened, and the security of the buyer's investment is enhanced, because of the unusual nature of cooperative financing. When an individual "buys" a

Attic dormers, either existing or added, increase the usable floor area of these two-story row houses by fifty percent.

cooperative, he purchases stock in the owning corporation, as outlined above. In fact, his "purchase price" buys the equivalent of an equity position. As an example, if a row house consists of five cooperative units, each selling at $30,000, and the building is mortgaged at $100,000 (i.e. $20,000 per unit), the purchaser is expected to pay $30,000 in cash and (essentially) he assumes a $20,000 mortgage (his portion of the total). Since most owners are not particularly interested in jeopardizing such a relatively large cash investment, an owner who defaults is rare. There are times, however, when an owner encounters personal financial difficulties and may have to be carried by the others in the corporation. But this does not present a major problem, since the "value" of his unit should be sufficient to insure eventual repayment.

The buyer of a cooperative does not receive a recordable and transferable deed, and since the stock he receives has limited marketability, even partial financing of the initial cash investment is complicated. In the example cited above the $30,000 necessary for the purchase of the cooperative unit would have to be paid in cash. While the purchaser can discuss with his banker possibilities of a loan to cover part of this purchase price, the bank generally will refuse to accept stock in the owning corporation as collateral for the loan. For all practical purposes the loan is made on the borrower's signature alone, or on the basis of other collateral acceptable to the lender. Some states are in the process of developing legislation to permit the use of the stock as collateral for the loan so this problem should ease in the future.

Once the cooperative purchaser has solved his problems of purchase, he can expect advantageous federal income tax deductions for his pro-rata share of the building's mortgage interest and taxes. In addition, if he should sublease his apartment, he is entitled to a deduction for depreciation. Generally these deductions exceed any profit made on the mark-up of rent charged to the interim occupant and provide a tax deduction as well. A cooperative owner considering the sublease of his unit should discuss his tax situation with an accountant to determine actual benefits, and such advice is even more important when an owner contemplates the sale of a cooperative unit.

Those considering the feasibility of buying a cooperative should first ascertain whether or not the project has been approved by any state agency whose approval may be required. Recently, these projects have come under close scrutiny in some cities because of the many problems experienced by occupants of large rent-controlled complexes where the owners have attempted to rid themselves of a financial burden by converting the building into a cooperative.

PARTNERSHIP

The partnership form of ownership is an emerging and interesting technique for row house renovation and is based on the concept of a group of friends or acquaintances banding together to solve mutual housing problems. Traditionally, cooperatives are conceived and executed by a sponsor or developer who sells the units at a profit when construction is almost complete. In contrast, partnerships are usually formed early in the construction process even before work on the building has been commenced. Depending on the legal entity created (a general or a limited partnership), all or some of the partners accept the various duties necessary to insure completion of the building in which all partners eventually live. The result is a building that has no developer's profit in its financial structure, and as a result, purchase prices of apartments are lower than those for equivalent cooperatives, and rents may be maintained below prevailing rental levels.

Advantages of Partnerships

1. The principal impetus behind the partnership form of ownership has been, logically, a financial one and the funds required from each party can be much lower than required for any other ownership form.
2. Partnerships are less formal than corporations and are consequently more suitable to small projects wherein tenant-owners may be friends.
3. When few individuals are involved in discussions leading to a partnership, it should be possible to secure an exception from fully registering the offering with the office of the state's Attorney General, thereby saving time and substantial legal expense.
4. Federal income tax benefits accruing from the deductibility of real estate taxes and mortgage interest are passed through the partnership direct to the partners, resulting in much less complicated accounting than that of a corporation.

Disadvantages Of Partnerships

1. Since a partnership does not have limited liability (except for limited partners of a limited partnership whose liability is limited to the extent of their investment in the partnership interest), the assets of the general partners may be exposed. For example, if damages are awarded in a liability suit, they may exceed the liability insurance coverage.
2. The transfer of a partnership interest from one owner to another is more difficult than the transfer of stock in a cooperative corporation. Even a well-planned partnership agreement may not cover all eventualities and may leave the incoming partner exposed to claims for an overcall, pro-rata payment of unforeseen expenses, etc.
3. Financing of the building may be more difficult than when another form of ownership is employed.

Under present legislation in New York City, for example, the owner of a rent-controlled building may evict a tenant provided need can be proven and the owner himself plans to occupy the room or apartment. Members of a number of partnerships in New York City have tried to use this legislation to their advantage by attempting to remove all tenants in a building on the premise that *all* owners plan to live there. This may spur many more partnerships into being, since the relocation of tenants is one of the most complex problems associated with row house renovations.

Whether a partnership, cooperative, or condominium is the correct vehicle for any given renovation project is a decision to be made by the project's lawyer after an evaluation of all the facts.

Chapter 5
Row House Management Prior to Renovation

Some row house buyers prefer a building which already has been vacated, particularly if there are plans for immediate reconstruction. While its initial purchase price will be higher than that of an occupied building, normal operating costs of the occupied building and the eventual expense of vacating the premises usually offset any purchase price differential. In the end both types of row houses — vacated or occupied — should cost the new owner approximately the same amount of money. Preference for either one or the other type depends entirely upon the individual buyer. The vacant building offers fewer problems but demands more cash, while the occupied building costs less and offers some measure of income but many more management problems.

This chapter concerns the occupied building because buyers usually purchase row houses which are occupied, since at the time an individual is in the market it may not be possible to find a vacant building which is entirely acceptable. While a building itself may be in excellent condition, the neighborhood may be undesirable, or vice versa, but if the prospective owner has sufficient capital and buys a building in good condition in a desired locality, there are advantages which accrue to the buyer of a tenanted row house. For example, there is a tax advantage resulting from the depreciation of the premises based on an estimate of the building's normal useful life. This enables the owner to deduct depreciation expense on his personal income tax return, thereby partially offsetting other income he may have as well as that derived from rental of the premises. Furthermore, the buyer is in a position to choose when he is able and when he wishes to start the reconstruction work, entirely dependent upon his financial position. Because of the many variables involved, under these circumstances it is advisable for an owner to obtain guidance from an accountant to determine the maximum benefits to be derived from the current tax laws, and also to learn what the tax consequences might be should he decide to sell at some later date.

Obviously, there are both advantages and disadvantages associated with purchasing an occupied row house. If the building is under rent-control (in one of the few cities where it still exists) it is highly questionable whether the new owner will be able to show any operating profit derived from rental income. In spite of the enthusiastic description and potential which a real estate broker may attach to the purchase, a new owner should be prepared to add funds to his original investment to offset operating losses, rather than optimistically expect a profit from rentals. Then when it comes time to vacate the building, prior to renovation, there will be additional expense.

If an occupied row house is purchased, there must be some control of operations, similar to the management of any piece of occupied real estate, and someone must be in charge; a manager in the guise of a superintendent is indispensable. It is the rare owner who is prepared to carry out and empty garbage cans on a daily basis, receive complaints from tenants any time of the day or night, or be responsible for electrical, plumbing, or any other type of repair. The average owner is employed and his office usually is located at some distance from his building. Even if he were willing to undertake all responsibilities which are part of a normal rental operation, he might not be in a convenient geographic position to do so. To successfully manage a row house with tenants, a part- or full-time superintendent is mandatory.

When a row house passes into the hands of a new owner, he may find that a superintendent, engaged by the former owner, is still associated with the building. At the time of purchase the new owner must decide whether this individual is to be retained or replaced by someone of his own choosing. There are several classes of superintendents: those who live rent-free in the building they manage and receive no compensation; those who live outside the building and receive some form of compensation; and those who live in a building rent-free and also receive some compensation because of their many responsibilities.

Usually it is advantageous to the new owner to retain the superintendent who managed the building prior to the change in ownership. Acquainted with all of the tenants, he is in a better position than any newcomer to continue amicable relations. Should tenant complaints arise, this man is better equipped to satisfactorily resolve the situation than a stranger. If and when the superintendent does not measure up to the new owner's expectations, however, he should be replaced immediately. If the individual lives in the building rent-free, there is no difficulty in removing him, since he probably does not enjoy the same rights as the other paying tenants. If he lives outside the house, then there is no problem other than actually discharging him. In either instance the new owner should be prepared to replace the man promptly with a competent, experienced superintendent since no building can operate efficiently without supervision.

Since the operation of an unrenovated row house necessarily must be considered a low budget investment (a fact which might be mentioned from time to time by the owner as a reminder to the superintendent that he should be constantly alert to controlling expenses), even an efficient

Peeling paint removed from the facade of two identical row houses reveals attractive and sound brick underneath. Note the air-conditioner location: possibly cooled air is ducted to the individual apartments.

superintendent cannot expect to receive more than nominal compensation. Responsibilities associated with his job are relatively minor, even when emergencies occur, since it is more than likely that the owner will engage a licensed electrician, plumber, or other mechanic should a serious problem arise. One way of ascertaining what the superintendent's compensation should be is to learn what the former owner had paid and be guided accordingly.

In general the salary varies according to the size of the building, the number of tenants, whether or not the superintendent lives rent-free, and what his actual responsibilities are. It is expected that those superintendents who live on the premises must attend to the refuse and garbage chores, see that the hallways are kept clean, tend the outside areas, make minor repairs, and collect rents. Those who live in, rent-free, and collect rents, but are responsible for nothing else, usually do not receive any salary. However, superintendents who live elsewhere and collect rents from the row house receive a compensation which averages between $600 to $1200 a year or more depending upon the number of rental units handled, the complexities associated with rent collections, etc.

OPERATING EXPENSE CONTROLS

An owner should expect to operate an occupied row house as he would any other type of business venture, thus controls are necessary. If management of the project is haphazard and inefficient the owner will incur losses, and he must rely upon his superintendent to see that the building is well managed and that operating costs are kept as low as possible. There are many ways in which the owner may assure himself of this cooperation. He must realize that he cannot be an absentee-landlord and automatically expect that his investment will show a profit based on correct rental income and accurate bills submitted by the superintendent. It is the owner's obligation to supervise the major phases of the building's operation and maintain close contact with the superintendent, not only to make certain that he is receiving the amounts due him, but that he is paying no more than the actual bills state.

This does not mean that the owner should treat his superintendent with distrust, nor does it mean that he badger him. However, there is a sensible difference between confidence and blind trust particularly when much of the income and expenses are in cash. It must be remembered that superintendents come in all sizes, types, and classes and some are more conscientious than others. It is the owner's obligation to select a man who measures up to the requirements of the job so he will not be cheated.

REPORTING FORMS

The owner's insistence on simple, easily filled-in reporting forms does much to facilitate his control of the building's management, and releases him from scrutinizing every item presented by the superintendent. The use of standard forms simplifies matters by insuring that identical information is being reported accurately in the same manner at the end of each designated period, thereby assisting both owner and superintendent. This makes week-to-week comparisons much easier for the owner.

Rent Forms (See Figure 2)

There may be two separate types of rent forms: for entire living units, usually rented on a monthly basis; and for single rooms, usually rented on a weekly basis. The owner should not find it difficult to prepare such forms, and the information expected should be confined to essentials such as room or apartment number, name of occupant, amount of rent paid, and the date of payment. If the owner wishes, he may maintain a consolidated report of these data for use in preparing tax returns. A simple procedure for the owner to follow is to lay out a form containing the above headings and then duplicate as many copies as may be required for the entire year. A handy supply in the superintendent's desk obviates any excuses for failure to fill out such forms when required.

Expense Forms (See Figure 3)

This form should be prepared in duplicate, one copy being retained by the superintendent, and one copy submitted to the owner for his records. This form controls operating expenses and should be a great aid to the owner, particularly when the superintendent understands that nothing will be paid unless clearly indicated and described on the Expense Form. It should be clearly understood by the superintendent that the owner must approve any expense over $10 or some other appropriate amount. This arrangement eliminates any involvement on the part of the owner in relatively minor repairs and still requires his approval for any large expenditure.

Since some superintendents have lucrative arrangements with repair services and often receive a kick-back when confronted with a major repair, the wise owner attends to the business arrangements himself. This avoids possible unpleasant argument, and the owner can be assured of paying a proper amount for services rendered. If the owner has the superintendent's confidence, and he believes that the man is honest, then there should be a petty cash arrangement by which minor charges may be handled. This petty cash amount should be checked from time to time, so that the superintendent can never assume that it serves as his personal fund.

As much as one might like to believe in the honesty of an employee, the very fact that the superintendent's job is a simple one, and relatively speaking there are no experience requirements, the caliber of the job often corresponds with the caliber of the man. Consequently, almost no owner can expect complete honesty from his superintendent; because of this fact, the wise owner closely supervises superintendent reports.

Figure 2
XX STREET ROW HOUSE COMPANY
Rent Record

Week Ending _____

Apt. No.	Tenant	Collected For This Week	Paid From To	Collected For Previous Wk.	Dates Paid	Security Deposit	TOTAL	Amt. Overdue	No. of Wks. Behind
1	Jones (Super)						No Rent		
2	Smith	10.00	12/30 1/6				10.00		
3	Johnson			25.00	12/26-1/2		25.00	25.00	1
4	Franklin			25.00	12/25-1/1		25.00	25.00	1
5	Sween	15.00	12/29 1/5				15.00		
6	Stephens	11.00	12/31 1/7	11.00	12/23-12/30		22.00		
7	Thomas	15.00	12/29 1/5				15.00		
8	Lee	15.00	12/29 1/5				15.00		
9	Cohen							45.00	3
10	Tuck	12.00	12/29 1/5				12.00		
11	Edwards	18.00	12/29 1/5				18.00		
12	Houser	10.00	1/03 1/10				10.00		
13	Eisenstern	15.00	12/30 1/6				15.00		
14	Goldstein (new)	10.00	1/02 1/9			10.00	20.00		
15	Sikes	15.00	12/30 1/6				15.00		
16	White	15.00	12/29 1/5				15.00		
17	Greene	15.00	12/28 1/4				15.00		
18	Grancis	17.00	12/30 1/6				17.00		
19	Richardson	10.00	1/01 1/8				10.00		
20	Wittenburg	10.00	12/31 1/7				10.00		
21	Coler	10.00	12/30 1/6				10.00		
	TOTALS	223.00	XXX XX	61.00	XXXXXX	10.00	294.00	95.00	XXX

Use This Space For Comments	LESS EXPENSES	19.00
	TOTAL DEPOSITED	275.00

1. Action being taken to disposses Cohen, Apt. 9, for nonpayment of rent.
2. $25 Petty Cash, carried forward.

Explanation of Sample Rent Record

Apartment 1	Superintendent lives rent-free.
Apartments 3 and 4	Tenants are 1 week delinquent in rent. Johnson had paid through 1/2 and Franklin through 1/1.
Apartment 6	Stephens was one week behind in rent, but is now current.
Apartment 9	Cohen has not paid rent this week and is now 3 weeks behind. (At the bottom of the page, under "Comments," the superintendent has noted that action has started to dispossess tenant.)
Apartment 14	Goldstein, who has just moved in, has given a security deposit in addition to 1 week's rent.

All other tenants are current.

Superintendent has $25 in petty cash for minor repairs, etc., when necessary after depositing the rent money and before collecting next week's rent. Column totals indicate that the owner is behind in rent by $95.00 and that $10.00 of the total should be deposited in his tenants' security deposit account.

Figure 3
XX STREET ROW HOUSE COMPANY
EXPENSES

Week Ending _____

	DESCRIPTION	TOTAL
Cleaning	Cleaning Entire Premises—Receipt Attached	$12.00
Repairs (Labor)	General Repairs—2 Hours	6.00
Laundry		
Housecleaning Items	House Cleansers	1.00
Hardware & Parts		
Other (Explain Below)		
	TOTAL	$19.00

DESCRIPTION OF REPAIRS—COMMENTS

Repairs: Sink trap, Room No. 5, replaced with spare, remove obstruction in third floor toilet.

Chapter 6
Relocation of Tenants

Tenant relocation is one of the most complex and nerve-wracking problems of row house ownership. Not only is this true in all cities where one or more tenants refuse to move when asked, but also in some cities the situation involves the statutory tenant, a product of rent control laws. Tenant relocation has plagued owners for years and the principal reasons are:

1. The tenancy and related inherent problems are unique to each building.
2. No one with relocation competence and experience has had the inclination to commit himself to paper to guide others.
3. Many of the techniques must be considered questionable or illegal.

The relocation problem is much less troublesome if each tenancy is covered by a valid lease. An examination of the appropriate lease clauses will indicate how to proceed and whether the tenant has any rights beyond the lease expiration. Many row house tenants occupy their space on a casual basis, and the lack of a lease may cause local statutes to apply and to relocate a tenant via these local procedures can be time-consuming indeed.

In rare instances a row house tenant will agree to move, when requested, and expect no compensation. This is the exception rather than the rule and the number is small. Perhaps no more than one tenant in every third row house could be classified in this category. Once a tenant hears that a building is to be vacated he often senses an opportunity for financial gain and must be dealt with in an entirely different manner. The owner needs a great amount of patience, a substantial amount of money, and often incentives must be provided before a stubborn tenant can be relocated. The cost of relocation can be substantial and the sum of $25,000 has been recorded as having been paid (by a commercial owner) to one individual before he was finally induced to leave. Fortunately, most row houses do not present such an extreme.

Generally the longer the owner is prepared to wait, and the more tenacious he appears to be, the less his relocation expense will be, but operating costs and carrying charges continue meanwhile. Although each tenant relocation must be handled individually, general solutions to the problem exist.

The most agreeable and effective relocations depend upon the cooperation and reasonableness of the tenant which is often complicated by a housing situation where demand exceeds supply, especially at the low rent levels required by individuals usually occupying unrenovated row houses. While alternate accomodations may be in short supply, they do exist. It is the owner's obligation to sufficiently motivate the tenant, so that he does locate substitute lodgings. This is where money plays an important, persuasive role. For a row house operating as a rooming house, a reasonable average budget of $2500 should be allotted for relocation expenses and payments to tenants with probable extremes of $500 and $5000 (high). For the average row house operating as an apartment house, the amounts will be somewhat higher, due to the greater likelihood of tenant families being larger.

A practical program, when tenants agree to cooperate, is as follows:

1. Upon taking title to the property the owner must determine when construction will begin. This is done by totaling all preconstruction time, such as that which will be devoted to architectural plans and decisions (usually the most time-consuming), legal arrangements, financing, and the complicated operation leading to the acceptance of a contractor's bid. Then, working backwards from the estimated construction start-date, 6 months should be allowed for relocation. If this happens to include any part of a winter season, additional time may be required, since it usually is more difficult to induce individuals to move in cold weather.
2. Next, current rents should be examined. If they are in excess of controlled, or registered rents, if such exist for the building, the owner should personally explain to each tenant what the adjusted amount will be, when it is payable and on what cycle, and to whom and where paid. If there is a superintendent or manager already responsible for the management of the building, he may be instructed to make the necessary arrangements. Most lawyers representing owners will urge, or even insist, that excessive rents be lowered to registered or legal levels at once. There is the danger that should the new owner continue to charge illegally high rents, he will subject himself to a lawsuit and a penalty which may equal three times the overcharge for the two prior years, or since the date of his ownership, plus lawyer's fees.
3. Delinquent rents should be dealt with promptly and firmly. This action can be handled by the owner himself, by the superintendent or agent, or by engaging a lawyer specializing in landlord-tenant law.

4. A careful analysis should be made of the tenancy to determine such facts as: total number of single rooms vs. total number of apartments; type of tenant, length of occupancy by each tenant; approximate age; which tenants have children or are on welfare; chronic troublemakers; etc. This type of survey enables the owner to better estimate what factors of relocation may be the knottiest to solve and he can plan accordingly.
5. The new owner should be prepared to offer alternate accommodations if a tenant should indicate an immediate willingness to move. He should make investigations among real estate brokers, friends, nearby superintendents, etc. as to vacant rooms or apartments which may be considered equivalent to those in his own building
6. In some instances, caseworkers of tenants on welfare occasionally are able to arrange for alternate accomodations that embody little or no charge to the owner.
7. Some tenants react favorably when there are inducements such as 1 or 2 weeks free rent, reimbursement for moving expenses, or permitting the tenant to take part or all of the furniture. (This item pertains to furnished rooms, and is an important factor in saving the owner expense of removal.) As a last resort, cash payments may be offered the tenant.

The intended purpose of the above approach to relocation is to insure amicable relations throughout the negotiations between owner and tenant and should avoid the necessity for any unpleasant tactics on either side and speed the move. Furthermore, should some legal complaint be lodged by the tenant, in spite of all reasonable efforts on the part of the owner, the judge should in no way be influenced to rule against the latter on the basis of tenant accusations.

There will be some tenants, as there always are in practically every building, who, in spite of the fact that they cannot possibly claim that the owner has committed some overt act, will balk at the move. Their objections may be supported by statements that they have not been able to find suitable quarters, or that they fear a new environment and new neighbors, or that they cannot meet moving expenses—or any number of excuses. With such tenants the owner or his agent should discuss not so much the question of personal problems, but what amount of money would be acceptable to assure their moving. When a sum has been agreed upon by both parties, the owner should make no payment until all furniture has been removed and the keys are in his possession. Should the tenant ask for a certain amount of time to make the move, an attempt should be made to have him sign a notice of intent to vacate. This will indicate how much he will receive to move, and when the move will occur. Although such an agreement usually is not enforceable in the courts, especially in the case of a statutory tenant, it still has some psychological value in favor of the owner.

By this time, with the start of construction imminent, the building will probably be incurring a monthly carrying charge of between $600 and $2500 depending upon its size and type of financing. To quibble over a relocation payment of $100 or even $300 is self-defeating; furthermore, if discussions are prolonged, it may prove to be more expensive then paying the monthly costs of a building which may be nearly vacant. This is the juncture where common sense plays a vital role, or when a good lawyer with a landlord-tenant practice is indispensable.

Should the owner be unsuccessful in persuading his tenants to vacate the premises on the basis of amicable negotiations, he has little choice other than to engage firms or agents specializing in this type of work to expedite matters. However, it must be remembered that in addition to whatever cash payments he will ultimately be compelled to make to tenants, and the legal fees incurred in the eviction process, the fees for these professional services are significant. If an owner is extremely fortunate, total eviction will occur within a 2- to 3- month period; in instances where there is prolonged legal action, it can take upwards of 2 years.

When considering relocation problems, harassment must be mentioned because some owners resort to such tactics. Any forms of coercion are precarious and most disagreeable; furthermore, such action usually proves the most expensive way to relocate tenants. The most valid argument against harassment of tenants, however, is its illegality.

Owners who harass their tenants become eligible for a reprimand from the city's department of housing at best. They may incur departmental action enforcing a reduction of the tenant's rent, while, at the same time, permitting the tenant to remain in possession of the premises. At worst the owner may subject himself to city-instituted legal action. When his building is located in an area subject to Urban Renewal control, the local Field Office will become involved—all of this in addition to any direct retaliation on the part of the irate tenant himself!

At the same time the tenant is seldom any such exception, and unfortunately when asked to move, some tenants react in particularly unpleasant ways. The tenant may destroy or mutilate parts of the building by physical force; he may deliberately damage, or stop up toilets and sinks to allow them to overflow; or he may from time to time throw breakable objects from the windows. He may even go so far as to threaten the owner with bodily harm. Additionally, there are other actions much less violent but just as effective, such as the refusal to pay rent, the organization of tenant committees to contest relocation efforts, and the institution of legal action sometimes based on trumped-up charges.

While such action on the tenant's part must be classed as reverse harassment, most of the owner's response must be considered as much of the same.
1. Instituting legal action for nonpayment of rent. While this may actually be true, there are possibilities of such legal action being

taken without actual support. Row house rents are often paid in cash so that the tenant has no legitimate way of disproving the owner's accusation unless he has a receipt.
2. Serving the tenant with an invalid eviction notice.
3. Removing laundry services, if any.
4. Cancelling maintenance, service, repairs, etc.
5. Removing locks and knobs from the front door of the building, thereby making it possible for vandals to enter.
6. Interrupting essential services, such as heat, hot water, gas or electricity.
7. Removing doors from bathrooms used by single-room tenants.
8. Disconnecting valves or cutting the pipes serving upper floors.

If a prospective buyer of a row house is not prepared to experience the preceding relocation problems, he might better consider another building. It *is* possible to buy one that has already been vacated by all tenants. The purchase price naturally will be higher. The owner himself must consider all the factors involved, what he will be obliged to do, its cost, etc., and then make his decision.

Chapter 7
Insurance: Prior to and During Construction

SELECTING AN INSURANCE BROKER

Row house buildings should be insured through a broker who is familiar with insuring small apartments and private residences. Large brokerage firms, while well equipped to handle almost any type of insurance coverage, generally favor the larger commercial accounts. A small building represents a smaller profit for the time invested, thus large brokerage firms are apt to prefer larger buildings. Owners should be wary of the part-time agent or broker, primarily because he may not be fully informed about current policy forms or market conditions, and he has little or no influence with insurance companies because of generally small premium volume. Such a relationship can lead to placement problems and poor claim service.

Usually a good broker will be recommended by a lawyer or a bank, and owners of other buildings represent a good source for recommendations. It is particularly important to determine how long a prospective insurance broker has been in business and with what companies he has accounts. In addition, an insurance broker may have to be licensed by the insurance department of the state. Essentially all brokers will charge the same rate for row house insurance, hence the insurance cost is not a determining factor in the choice of a broker. It should be noted, however, that some Mutual companies provide a dividend which may be deducted in advance, often amounting to 10% of the premium.

An insurance broker does not usually demand fees or other charges for his services; he is compensated entirely by commissions that are paid by the insurance company. While there are standard forms of commissions for different types of policies, usually there are no differences in policy cost to the insured, regardless of who the broker may be.

The designation "insurance broker" may not be appropriate in the reader's area; such an individual works exclusively for the insured. Not only does he owe no allegiance to any particular company, but he buys insurance which he considers the best for his customer. On the other hand an "agent" is the representative of a particular company, thus he is apt to be somewhat partial to his company in accepting certain types of insurance.

BASIC INSURANCE COVERAGES FOR ROW HOUSES

The principal insurance policy required by a row house owner is the multiperil policy. This policy provides the following coverages:

1. Building and contents, consisting of fire and extended coverage (i.e. windstorm, explosion, riot, vandalism, and malicious mischief). It also covers machinery and equipment used in the operation of the building, but does not cover personal property (except building property, such as lobby furniture).
2. Rental income insurance may be included in a multiperil policy. This provision reimburses the owner for unrentability of an apartment as the result of a fire, thereby insuring continual income in the event of a loss.
3. Public liability insurance protects the owner against damages awarded to others, due to the operation or existence of the building.

Although these coverages can be obtained separately, there is approximately a 15% saving when purchased jointly. Among those in the insurance field this type of insurance policy is frequently referred to as a "package policy."

Liability insurance premiums are determined by geographic area, together with the total square footage in the building that is to be covered. For a policy with limits of $100,000 for each person, and $300,000 for each accident, the average premium is about $4.00 per 100 square feet of floor space. The premium can vary 50% more or less depending upon the location of the building.

CO-INSURANCE

The 80% Co-Insurance Clause is a warranty in fire and extended coverage policies whereby the insured agrees that he will carry insurance equal to at least 80% of the value of the property. When his coverage falls below the 80% level, the owner becomes a co-insurer and the following example will emphasize the hazards when an owner unwittingly becomes a co-insurer. Assuming the value of a building to be $100,000, at least $80,000 of insurance must be carried. Were the owner to carry only $40,000 and a $10,000 loss occurred, the owner will have been deemed to be self-insuring one-half of the risk. As a consequence, the insurance company would provide only $5,000 of the $10,000 loss. Had the loss been total, the insurance company would pay only $40,000.

Fire insurance premiums are also set by geographic area, although specific buildings may be rated individually. The minimum rate for this coverage of masonry apartment buildings with five or more families is around 40 cents

Two extremes side-by-side: A stucco-faced row house with Dutch overtones, and a two-story building of wood-frame construction, hardly ever found in cities today due to the perpetual maintenance required and susceptibility to fire.

per hundred dollars of value per year for fire, extended coverage, and vandalism. A savings may be made by purchasing 3-year coverage, with the rate often being 2.7 times the yearly rate. The same 15% reduction for a package policy applies in this instance.

Premiums for rental insurance are generally 60% of the fire insurance rate.

OTHER TYPES OF INSURANCE

1. Workmen's Compensation Insurance to cover building employees (e.g. janitors, superintendents, etc.). A State Compensation Board may require that such coverage must be carried if the job is full time, *or* if the occupation might be adjudged hazardous (a probable designation of the work performed by these people). The premium is usually 3 to 4% of annual payroll.

2. Disability Benefits Coverage costs approximately $30 per year per employee and covers an employee who is injured off the job.

3. Fidelity Bonds are usually recommended if an employee handles cash (i.e. collection of rents) during the course of his work.

4. If the building is equipped with a sprinkler system, sprinkler leakage insurance should be carried.

5. Specialized coverages are available for specific risks, such as plate glass coverage. These special types must be individually discussed with a broker.

SURVEY OF INSURANCE

Any reputable insurance broker will be willing to survey the insurance situation of a particular building. This consists of making an analysis of the insurance covering the building at the time of purchase, together with recommendations of adequate coverage that should also be provided. Such a survey may be conducted in the following manner:

1. The risk is studied according to: type, current occupancy, and the eventual plans for the building after renovation has been completed.
2. Exposures are identified as to: fire, extended coverage, vandalism, theft, rents, etc.
3. A basic insurance program is then established.

Such a survey might uncover the fact that inadequate insurance is currently being carried on the property or that insurance is carried on property not owned, especially if existing insurance is acquired at the time of purchase, or when several brokers are involved.

INSURANCE REQUIRED OF THE CONTRACTOR

Contractors can be expected to provide certificates of insurance to either the owner or the architect. These certify that the contractor carried certain coverages pertaining to the following risks:

1. Public Liability Insurance, covering the contractor's operations. This includes completed operations insurance which covers injuries arising after the contractor has completed the work. (For example, plaster falling and injuring a bystander.) The insurance broker who covers the building for the owner should review the limits of insurance carried by the contractor and indicate whether or not, in his opinion, such limits are sufficient. It is suggested that minimum limits be $100,000 for each person, and $300,000 for each accident.
2. Property Damage Insurance should be carried for damage to property (e.g. adjacent buildings).
3. The contractor's employees must be covered by Workmen's Compensation Insurance. If such coverage is not current and one of the contractor's employees is injured on the job, the owner may become liable not only for the award, but for a fine as well.
4. The contractor should also have automobile (truck) liability insurance.

INSURANCE DURING CONSTRUCTION

A row house under construction is usually covered by a type of insurance known as Builder's Risk Completed Value. Essentially the policy is the same as that used for a completed building, with the additional clause inserted that the building is in the course of reconstruction and the privilege of completion is granted. Such a policy is written at the completed building rate, and the premium does not increase as work is performed.

INSURANCE BINDERS

Policies acquired with a building may not adequately cover all the risks being assumed by the owner. If additional coverage is required, the broker will discuss such coverage with an underwriter, and after reaching agreement, the broker will issue a binder covering such risks. The binder serves as a temporary policy and itemizes all details of the insurance to be issued. A binder is superseded by the issuance of the actual policy.

INSURANCE LOSSES

The size of an insurance brokerage firm has significant influence upon how a loss will be handled. When a broker has a reasonable account with an insurance company and a loss occurs, there probably will be little question of whether or not the loss is covered, mainly because the policy language is specific, but a broker in a sound position with his company may arrange a somewhat more advantageous settlement for his client. In some cases a public adjuster (an independent firm) serves a useful purpose, especially in a commercial loss (e.g. business interruption): but most row house losses are reasonably standard, and the services of the broker should suffice.

In the event of a loss the burden of proving the value both before and after the loss rests on the insured. Because of this responsibility, the owner is urged to retain a set of the building plans, together with canceled checks to support any possible claim.

Adequate fire insurance coverage for some row houses occasionally is difficult to obtain because of natural fire hazards, deteriorated condition of the building, fire losses in the immediate neighborhood, etc. In such instances the broker will attempt to arrange with two or more companies to divide the coverage by writing separate policies. When a broker is unable to obtain fire insurance for a specific building, he may apply to the state property underwriting association for an assignment of the risk to a member of the association. This assigned risk "pool" is a vehicle established by insurance companies in some states, whereby a risk unacceptable through regular channels is assigned sequentially to a member company. In fact, insurance on a building might be assigned to the very company that refused the original request.

Personal property insurance is discussed in Chapter 20.

Chapter 8
Legal Aspects of Row House Renovation

LAWYER'S AREAS OF RESPONSIBILITY

The lawyer has the responsibility for the legal aspects of the successive stages of a row house project. These phases may include:

1. Advice, based on proposed post-renovation use and occupancy, as to the legal form in which the building should be acquired and held, its tax aspects, and legal relationships between co-owners.
2. Acquiring the property.
3. Vacating the building after purchase, if required.
4. Representing the new owner's interest with old tenants who remain after purchase or with new tenants after renovation.
5. Complying with the legal requirements for renovation financing.
6. Negotiating or reviewing agreement with the architect or contractor.
7. Handling problems with government agencies.

These aspects are separate but interrelated. For example, among other considerations, the form of legal ownership used may dictate the extent, type and availability of financing, as well as ultimate rents.

There are, however, business and personal decisions a lawyer should not be expected to make; questions, for example, of whether or not row house living will coincide with the personal preferences of the prospective owners, or, after appropriate discussion, whether an owner can actually afford to purchase, renovate, and carry the costs of a particular building.

FINDING A LAWYER

As a minimum, the prospective buyer should select a lawyer with a real estate background. Broad legal experience or prior involvement in one or more completed renovations is most advantageous as row house legal problems may range from technical aspects of federal government programs and procedures through real estate, corporation, partnership, and tax law, to eviction proceedings. Equally important as the choice of a lawyer is for the prospective owner to consult with him as early as possible, even in the "thinking about it" stage of the project. A good source of legal assistance is the personal recommendation of an owner who has successfully completed a renovation.

It is most important that the lawyer and the purchaser have the ability to adapt to each other's points of view, that the buyer have confidence in the lawyer, and that there be the fullest cooperation between them. Should major differences appear, the relationship should be dissolved.

FEES

It is often difficult for people without prior experience in working with lawyers to understand the payment of what may appear to be substantial sums for services instead of for "bricks and mortar." It is, moreover, practically impossible to obtain a precise advance quotation of fees, especially when a purchaser is interested not only in the lawyer's negotiating the acquisition of the property, but also expects to receive assistance throughout the entire project. A lawyer with row house renovation experience should, however, be able to quote a range of fees with a basic hourly charge as a guide. Also, some itemization is possible according to the phase of work involved such as: a fee for acquiring the building, for advice and assistance in the financing phases, etc. The purchaser should inquire and be made aware of the possible range of these costs well in advance, subject to extra allowances for unexpected problems.

ACQUIRING THE ROW HOUSE

The lawyer's role in the purchase of a row house is not much different from that which he plays when he represents a client buying any other residential building. Once the decision to purchase has been made, he must make certain that the agreed transaction is completed and title is acquired, subject to whatever tenancies, mortgages, violations, and other legal and physical conditions that may be agreed to by the buyer and seller.

When title is conveyed (usually referred to as "the closing of title" or simply "the closing"), the purchaser expects to receive clear marketable title to the property. This is a necessity, as no lending institution will finance the renovation without it. Fortunately, in major cities where turnover of property is frequent, title flaws have usually been smoothed out during the preceding years in which the property has passed from owner to owner. To make certain of such protection, in many cities the purchaser's lawyer usually arranges to procure title insurance in the amount of the purchase price, with the purchase contingent on the issuance of such coverage. The rates for title insurance are fixed by law with the insuring companies licensed

Old fixtures fit well with new decorative wallpaper in this row house bathroom complete with wooden seat. (Photo © 1979 by Jim Kalett)

by the state, and the premium paid only once. In addition, the lending institution will require mortgage title insurance in the loan amount.

The basic document in the purchase is the contract, which is usually prepared by the seller's lawyer. He often uses as a framework a title company's printed form as most lawyers understand the meaning of its standard provisions. The contract contains the exact terms of the transaction, including:

1. The purchase price and method of payment (including cash and purchase money mortgage, if any).
2. A legal description of the property.
3. The property's legal condition (i.e. if it is being purchased subject to mortgages).
4. The property's physical condition (i.e. the existence of violations of record and if or how they are to be disposed of prior to closing, or if the property is being purchased "as is").
5. The terms of any mortgages that will remain liens on the premises when title is acquired.
6. Whether the building will be free of tenancies and provisions, if any, for vacancies as may occur prior to closing.
7. Provisions for purchase or disposition of personal property in the building.
8. What happens if various defined problems cannot be resolved.
9. The date, place, and time of closing.

One usually negotiated provision concerns the amount of cash deposit by the purchaser at the time of signing the contract and whether or not such sum will be held in escrow (i.e. in "trust," usually by the seller's lawyer) until the closing or paid to the seller, in which event he may use it as he wishes. This payment is generally 10% of the total purchase price, but may vary depending upon the length of time until closing. As a matter of law, the buyer may have a lien on the property to the amount of such deposit. However, with a seller of unknown financial ability it is often prudent to escrow the deposit, rather than risk the disproportionate expense, trouble, and delay of a lien foreclosure action for the relatively small amount involved.

Another negotiated provision may be the amount and terms of the purchase money mortgage. This device is required as banks are often unwilling to make purchase money loans on row houses due to their poor location or condition. This is in contrast to suburban home purchases where the buyer usually can induce a bank to make a large purchase money mortgage loan, use the proceeds of such loan to pay off existing mortgages, and with any excess, plus additional funds, pay the balance of the purchase price in cash. The row house seller accommodates the buyer and often makes the transaction possible by accepting a purchase money mortgage as part of the total purchase price in an amount equal to the difference between the cash payment and the mortgages that remain on the premises after closing.

The terms of such purchase money mortgage, including its interest rate, amortization, and whether or not it will be subordinated to future financing that may be required for renovation, are usually the subject of negotiation between the parties and their lawyers. The seller's willingness to subordinate is very valuable to the purchaser particularly when he is thinly financed, and it is discussed in Chapter 12, Financing.

Generally between 30 and 60 days elapse between the signing of the contract and the closing of title. This may vary depending upon such factors as requirements to vacate, time involved for title companies to make title and violation searches, or the need for a seller-occupant to find other living accommodations. Generally the parties are each entitled to a reasonable adjournment to clear up problems that the title company may uncover or to allow the buyer to complete financing arrangements.

Vacating the row house is a thorny problem in some cities due to rent control laws which apply to many such buildings and give possessory rights at low rents to tenants except for such things as nonpayment of rent. In most cases the buyer will need a completely vacant building before he can begin renovation. Accordingly, it becomes a matter of bargaining with the seller as to how vacant the building must be at closing, with a premium often being paid for vacancies. Purchase of a partially vacant building results in low income, continuing fixed expenses, probable financial losses, and difficulties of dealing with what may develop into a hard core of recalcitrant occupants. Because of these difficulties some lawyers advise against buying other than a completely vacant building when the owner anticipates commencing renovation relatively soon after his purchase.

The proposed contract is then reviewed by the purchaser and his lawyer. In all probability changes will be negotiated, additional problems defined, solutions provided, and final refinements made of the details of the transaction. Once this by now tailor-made document is approved by the parties, it is signed, becomes binding, and gives rise to various rights in the event of performance or nonperformance.

On receipt of the title report by the buyer's lawyer, he sends the seller's lawyer a copy of the sheet from the report setting forth exceptions to the insuring of title, the description of the property that the company will insure, and any other important information such as open violations, liens, and unpaid taxes. The seller's lawyer then takes steps to eliminate the exceptions on the report, and the parties, their lawyers, and representatives of the title company, the broker, and any lending institutions appear at the appointed time and place for closing.

At the closing, following final review of the papers presented by both sides, the seller delivers the deed, the buyer executes the purchase money note and mortgage and pays the balance of the cash, reduced or increased slightly by adjustments as of the closing date of ongoing expenses, such as fuel, insurance, taxes and of rental income. The title company brings its searches to date by telephone, omits any exceptions to insuring title, and takes the deed and mortgage for recording. As part of the closing details, based on papers prepared by his lawyer, the buyer notifies tenants as to the location of their security deposits and advises the tenants and various mortgagees and government agencies of the change in ownership. The buyer's lawyer then prepares a closing statement for his client outlining the financial details of the transaction. He may also write a letter describing the legal ramifications of the closing accompained by copies of closing documents.

POSTCLOSING MATTERS

During the interim between closing and completion of financing arrangements and renovation, the areas of landlord-tenant relations and building violations are of most concern to the owner's lawyer. The eventual objective of the new owner is to see that his building becomes vacant so that renovation may commence. In some areas the building's managing agent or owner must be registered with the municipality, and the premises made or kept free of violations. If, after an inspection, violations are placed on the building and are not corrected, criminal proceedings may be instituted against the owner and his lawyer's responsibility to solve these problems, often disproportionately expensive to the amount of money involved. They are, in addition, often wasteful, as money is often required to be spent on temporarily correcting conditions that will disappear in the building renovation.

OWNERSHIP METHODS

The legal form in which title to the property is held illustrates the breadth of problems that confront the row house lawyer. The choice of such form arises from the proposed use of the building and gives rise to a host of financial and tax complexities. An individual may hold title in his own name; other possibilities include a corporation, a cooperative corporation, a general or limited partnership, or a condominium. Many factors influence the choice and each must be carefully weighed.

Individual

The owner holding title in his own name, or named as a general partner where the partnership holds title, subjects himself to unlimited personal liability. This makes all of his current and future assets available if there is a successful uninsured claim against him (e.g. in the event of damage to a third party resulting from fire in the building). Furthermore, tax factors and insurance against contingencies, which must be in large amounts these days, may outweigh the risks.

Corporate Ownership

This limits liability to the corporation's assets. Under very limited circumstances, Subchapter S of the Internal Revenue Code may apply, and expense items may be offset against the owner's other income.

Cooperatives and Condominiums

These forms of ownership are covered in Chapter 4. Lending institutions in some areas do not have much experience with the condominium form of ownership and may be reluctant to finance the relatively small number of units in a renovated row house in such manner.

MISCELLANEOUS LEGAL SITUATIONS

Financing

When the new row house owner begins making plans to finance his proposed renovation, he may turn to his lawyer for assistance. Through his acquaintance with lending institutions, the lawyer may serve as a broker between lender and owner for which services he is entitled to a fee beyond his charges for legal services. Based on plans and specifications, a contractor's bid, and its own appraisal and evaluation, the lender issues a letter of commitment setting forth the terms under which it is prepared to make the loan, the time within which the commitment must be accepted, and the time of completion. Generally, construction loans bear a high interest rate due to the risk that the owner may run out of money, or for other reasons may abandon the project, in which event the lender will be forced to spend its own funds and complete the building and then sell or operate it to achieve repayment of its loan. Accordingly such loans are of short duration with sharp increases in interest rates if they are not repaid as agreed. Although the lawyer for the lending institution will prepare the loan documents, the owner's lawyer must review them and be certain that legal requirements on the owner's side are met prior to the mortgage closing. The basic documents for such closing usually include a building loan agreement setting forth the sums that may be drawn down at various phases of construction, a mortgage note, and a first mortgage.

Some lenders only make long-term permanent loans, and the owner may have to secure construction money from another source based on the replacement or "take out" of the construction lender by the permanent mortgagee. Some institutions will make a construction loan which is converted into a permanent loan on completion. Or, the owner may proceed with renovation and attempt to arrange for permanent financing during construction, a much riskier course.

Federal Government Guaranteed Mortgages and Real Estate Tax Relief

There are a variety of available government insured mortgage programs, depending upon the location of the property, type of renovation, etc. Because the statutory interest rates of such programs are generally below the market rate, the lender may charge "points" or a discount so that in total cost such loans may be as expensive as conventional loans. Moreover, procedures are strictly regulated and very involved. Such financing may, however, offer possibilities for financing projects for which funds are otherwise unavailable and may also offer large and long-term mortgages and in some instances partially pay various costs, such as architect's and lawyer's fees, interest during construction, taxes and insurance that the owner is normally required to pay at a time when the building is in construction and producing no income.

In New York and a few other cities relief may be available from real estate tax payments for a number of years after renovation provided the building is rehabilitated from a substandard condition. The availability of such relief depends also on the work done and the willingness of the owner to accept controlled rentals during the period of the relief. This requires very careful record keeping by the owner.

Chapter 9
The Architect

Whatever way one describes the functions of an architect, he stands at the center of the building process. It is his responsibility to coordinate the diversified interests of the individuals involved in a manner that provides proper and expeditious means for completing the project.

SELECTING AN ARCHITECT

The selection of the architect may well be one of the two or three most important decisions an owner makes when planning a renovation. By that decision he will have chosen both a designer and a professional advisor, and he will enter into a relationship that normally lasts for 6 to 18 months. Early in this period the architect must acquaint himself with the owner's needs and ideas so that he may be able to translate them into tangible form. In addition to a consideration of "bricks and mortar," the architect must be familiar with the owner's personal attitudes and reactions concerning family, neighbors, and even neighborhood, since these factors also influence the final design.

The architect is either selected directly, or he is accepted on the basis of recommendations. A direct selection depends upon the owner's initiative, and he chooses the architect who appears to be the best qualified. Usually the owner who is contemplating a complete renovation will select an individual whose style and ideas he admires and respects. Or he may depend upon the opinion of a third party, one who has had personal dealings with a particular architect and where the results have been satisfactory.

Information about architects who are interested in row house renovations may be obtained from the following sources:

1. Local Chapters of the American Institute of Architects (A.I.A.) will furnish names of eligible architects.
2. The current interest in row house renovation has spurred the publication of articles which describe such projects and include the names

of the architects involved. Typical articles are to be found in: *House Beautiful, House and Garden*, and *American Home* among others.
3. Professional architectural publications such as *Architectural Record* occasionally contain articles describing renovations of an exceptional nature, and mention the architect's name.
4. Many row house neighborhoods have sponsored house tours which include renovated buildings. The names of architects responsible for these buildings may be obtained while on tour.
5. Other owners often provide referrals.

HOW THE ARCHITECT ASSISTS THE OWNER

If an owner is to be satisfied, the building plan he chooses must reflect his taste, his needs, and his budget. Since many people are impulsive and allow their emotions to override other considerations, it is wise to consult with an architect from the outset of planning. The architect can advise what changes in an existing building are possible, what the renovation cost will probably be, determine whether a building is structurally sound, and he can evaluate the existing mechanical systems. Moreover, to work with an architect *before* purchasing a building offers several additional advantages. First, it allows the client sufficient time to form an opinion of the architect before retaining him for the final design. He has the opportunity to test the architect's ideas and satisfy himself that they may be coordinated with his own. To change architects after a contract has been signed and design work initiated can prove awkward and unpleasant. Second, it permits the architect to become familiar with his client's needs prior to selecting a building. The architect is in a position to make recommendations that may not only save money, but that can benefit the design. The architect is better equipped to recognize physical potential than is the owner: how a building is located, whether on the north or south side of the street, how deep and wide it may be, whether there is a rear extension and of how many stories, the building's entrance, whether at the street level or by means of a stoop, etc. All of these factors influence layout and design.

A client interested in disturbing a building's original features as little as possible must be willing to accommodate his needs to the situation. While this may pose certain personal inconveniences, he must realize that unless he is prepared to make a considerable outlay of money, plaster moldings, intricately carved woodwork, elaborately designed jambs or bases, and original tiles, once removed, can never be properly replaced, and if damaged are almost impossible to repair.

RELATIONSHIP BETWEEN ARCHITECT AND OWNER

The architect's responsibilities are directly related to the community in which he practices and to the client by whom he is retained. He must be

The steep stair angle of this brick row house is a clue that it was fit tightly on the lot and probably originally housed servants for the grander row houses located nearby.

thoroughly familiar with the codes and regulations that will affect his design. His design must be sensitive to its surroundings, and ideally any modifications or additions of an external nature should complement and enhance the general character of a neighborhood.

The architect must assist with the preparation of a detailed listing of the owner's requirements, translate them into a preliminary design, and further develop this preliminary design into one which, when finished, will be acceptable to the owner. Next, he will prepare the construction documents essential to conveying the design intention to a contractor, superintend the bidding of several reliable contractors, and finally, supervise the construction until its successful completion in accordance with the contract documents.

The owner, as a party to contracts with both architect and contractor, assumes certain responsibilities which he is expected to discharge promptly and reasonably. The owner must candidly discuss the finances involved, and be able to assist the architect in resolving possible conflicts between his budget and the desired program. Although it is usual practice for the architect to review each contractor's application and certify that payment is due before payment is made, the owner will be expected to pay both architect and contractor promptly as outlined in the contract documents.

The owner must recognize that in renovation work the unexpected can happen and that in his interpretation of the construction documents, the architect must be reasonable and fair to both the owner and the contractor. If a disagreement arises between the owner and the architect which requires the intercession of a third party, usually the dispute is taken before the American Arbitration Association. Its services are available to investigate and provide an impersonal decision.

The drawings and specifications prepared by the architect usually remain his property and the information they contain can be used at other locations by the owner only with the architect's authorization.

AGREEMENT BETWEEN ARCHITECT AND OWNER

There should always be a written contract between the architect and the owner. Since verbal agreements can lead only to misunderstandings, a written contract in the form of a letter or a formal document is preferable. As a rule, the architect chooses the appropriate A.I.A. pre-printed document, one which is generally recognized by the legal profession as an acceptable and valid basis for agreement between the two parties.

COMPENSATION OF THE ARCHITECT

An architect is compensated for his services according to the type and scope of the work involved. The basis for this compensation is usually determined by one of the following methods.

Percentage of the Construction Cost

This is the most common form of agreement between architect and owner and is particularly suitable to a project such as a row house renovation where the scope of the project can be defined and where the architect's services are required throughout the construction phase. While such contract may be drawn by the owner and the architect, or by their legal representatives, it is usual practice to employ A.I.A. document B-131 (Standard Form of Agreement Between Owner and Architect). This form enumerates the responsibilities of the architect and allows for amendment or inclusion of additional conditions as required.

The percentage fee suggested by the A.I.A. for alteration work, handled with a single lump sum construction contract, is 15% for the first $100,000 and 14% for the next $150,000 of cost. These percentages happen to be the highest suggested for any type of construction and take into account the very involved nature of alteration work. In the case of a warehouse, or factory, for example, a fee of 6% is suggested, while work on a custom residence would result in a fee of 12%. These percentages are merely suggestions, and it should be recognized that there may be variances according to the extent and type of work demanded. Considerably lower fees are quoted by architects who omit one or more of the usual architectural duties. In such instances the owner is usually competent to undertake the omitted work himself (supervision of construction, for example).

The owner's budget for renovation may not always prove sufficient and may require upward revision. When this occurs, both the owner and architect may agree on a limit, or "upset" figure, which determines the largest total construction expenditure upon which the architect's percentage may be based. This has the advantage of permitting the client to determine exactly the architect's fee, even though he may not be able to control the contractor's bid, nor the final renovation costs.

In addition to his regular fees the architect is normally reimbursed for items such as transportation (when the construction site is located at some distance from his office), long distance telephone calls, architectural models, plan and specification reproductions, special technical consultation services (consulting engineers, soil tests), etc.

Multiple of Direct Personnel Expense

The basis for this type of agreement is A.I.A. document B-211 (Multiple of Direct Personnel Expense) and involves periodic payment for professional services. Payments to architects, draftsmen and engineers are totaled according to the actual hours worked, with the addition of such normal expenses as workmen's compensation, disability insurance, etc. This type of agreement is used infrequently for renovation work but it is applicable to projects of indefinable scope and to those where the architect is engaged to provide only partial or limited services. Since the fee depends upon a multiple of the actual cost of these services and not on the cost of renovation, the architect is required to maintain an accurate time record, available for inspection by the owner.

Professional Fee Plus Expense

When there is no need to prepare any technical drawings or specifications, although some of the architect's services are required, A.I.A. document B-311 (Professional Fee Plus Expense) applies and the amount of the fee is usually negotiated.

Document B-311 is used frequently as an agreement between owner and architect preceding the purchase of a row house. Later, when a building has been acquired, the two parties agree to change to Document B-131 (Percentage of Construction Cost), which makes provisions for actual construction.

PAYMENT OF FEES

Payments to the architect, according to the most often used Percentage of Construction Cost Agreement, are as follows. The architect receives 5% of the projected fee as a retainer upon execution of the agreement. An additional 30% is paid for the design phase, divided into two payments: 10% for the schematic design phase after the program has been established, and 20% for the design development phase which explores the final design in depth. The preparation of the working drawings accounts for a further 40%; payments during this phase are usually made in monthly installments. After the bids are in, and an award has been made to a contractor, the architect receives another 5%. If necessary, the fee is adjusted at that time to reflect an actual rather than an estimated cost. Payments continue on a monthly basis during the construction phase with the final payment made on substantial completion of the construction work. In the case of row house renovation substantial completion is interpreted as the issuance of a new Certificate of Occupancy.

The architect receives payment for Direct Personnel and Reimbursable Expenses monthly, upon presenting detailed invoices. Under the Professional Fee Plus Expense contract, the architect's fee is paid in the same manner as when the Percentage of Construction Cost of the Project is used.

Obviously, the above payments can be modified by agreement to concur with the financial characteristics of the project.

Chapter 10
The Architect's Role

The design of a major renovation should be a challenging and rewarding experience for both owner and architect. While it is not always possible to include in a renovation as many of the elements of design as would ordinarily be incorporated in a new building (such as special siting, exterior treatment, or new structural systems), within the parameter of existing party walls there still is ample opportunity to test an architect's ingenuity in his use of space, light, texture and color. This assumes, naturally, that the owner is personally interested in a building which is more than merely a financial vehicle.

THE PROGRAM

The first step toward the design of a renovation is the preparation of a program which defines the living pattern and arrangement of the building most acceptable to the owner. The more carefully thought out and complete the program, and the better understood by both owner and architect, the more successful the final design is apt to be. The architect assists and encourages the owner to reveal his ideas so that they may develop and be incorporated into the final design. For the architect to impose his own views at this stage is a mistake; his primary obligation is to interpret the client's desires in three dimensions.

Some typical program considerations are:

1. The number of rooms the owner will require.
2. The type and number of rental apartments.
3. The location of the owner's apartment within the building and its relationship to the garden, to the building entry, and to the tenant's apartments.
4. Relationship of the rooms within the apartment, especially as this affects privacy, flow of space, and convenience provided by vertical and horizontal circulation.
5. The size and character of the individual rooms.
6. Building security.

SCALED PLANS

At the same time that the program is prepared the architect will also prepare scaled plans of the building as it is currently laid out, should they not already exist. These plans are usually drawn at 1/4 inch to the foot, and they provide an effective means for recognizing on paper some relationships which might otherwise escape notice. This is often true when a room is cluttered with debris, or when a particularly outstanding detail may overshadow other features in the room. A study of these scaled drawings, however, should be balanced by frequent visits to the building to substantiate impressions.

THE LAYOUT, OR DESIGN

Once a program has been established and scaled drawings prepared, the architect draws a layout indicating the requisite number of rooms with consideration of their use and relationship. There are times when the first layout will substantially meet the requirements of the program and only a minimal amount of refinement will be required, but this is more apt to happen with minor renovations. Normally, however, the presentation of several layouts is required before the final arrangement is determined. Since the owner naturally expects the best possible arrangement for his building, his natural impatience must be weighed against the satisfaction which should come from an excellent final design.

The most essential ingredient of a good design is a natural order of circulation. This is true of any architectural project, but can be uniquely so in the case of a row house where the general disposition of the rooms is already established, and vertical circulation — separate from the public halls and stairs — often is the major element of design. A new stairway offers an opportunity to explore interior space and tests the architect's inventiveness.

Unless the problem that confronts the architect is planning on a vertical order — a house on a steep site, for example — the layout is largely a two-dimensional study. A premature concern for three-dimensional aspects of a design may undermine some of the clarity of the layout, and there are times when a charming vignette may obscure the legitimate needs of the client. Not until the layout has been properly established will the architect seriously explore its value by means of sectional drawings, perspective drawings, and possible cardboard models. Frequently an owner will ask to see a finished model or a set of presentation perspectives earlier than the architect considers feasible. It is customary for the architect to receive additional compensation for such work.

At this juncture a contractor is asked to examine the plans to offer a preliminary estimate of construction cost. The contractor should be in a position to state whether or not he thinks the proposed design will

Interior rooms can be enhanced by exposing existing brick walls.
(Photo © 1979 by Jim Kalett)

significantly exceed the owner's budget. As reluctant as contractors usually are to give any estimates in the absence of finished drawings and specifications, even a rough indication of cost can prove valuable.

BUILDING DEPARTMENT AND BUILDING PERMIT

Before any new construction can be undertaken the building department must issue a building permit, so as soon as the design phase has been completed, the architect submits the plans and necessary forms that describe the extent of all new work to the department. If space is to be added to the building, zoning calculations may have to be prepared, indicating compliance with prevailing regulations. A waiting period after filing is normal before the architect can expect to receive either notice of approval or a list of objections which must be satisfactorily answered prior to approval. A building permit can then be issued upon application by a contractor and the payment of a permit fee.

In some cities multiple dwellings (buildings with three or more dwelling units) receive much closer scrutiny from the building department and must pass much more stringent fire standards requirements than one- or two-family dwellings. For multiple dwellings filing plans and answering objections posed by the building examiner can prove to be an extraordinarily frustrating and time-consuming experience. For the larger renovation it may be wise to retain an "expeditor" to file the plans with the building department. This individual is familiar with department personnel and procedures, and frequently can save the architect and the owner weeks, if not months of valuable time. The expeditor's fees are incurred on an hourly basis and are usually assumed by the owner.

Once the plans are approved, they are submitted in duplicate or triplicate. One set is retained by the department, one set may be issued to the building inspector who is assigned to periodically visit the construction site to insure that the actual construction complies with the plans, and one approved set is given to the contractor before he begins work. This last set must be kept on the job throughout the construction period.

BUILDING CODES

Nearly all construction projects are governed by one or more building codes which have been established to protect the public. Walter F. Aikman, a building code expert, informs us that "Laws to protect the owner and others from faulty construction have existed for centuries. The penal code of Hammurabi, King of Ancient Babylon, 2250 B.C., contained the first known building code. This code of six short sentences stipulated the builder's wage, which, in terms of measurement today, was about 10 cents per square foot. The other five sentences prescribed penalties if the house was not built to the requirements of firmness, including death to the builder if faulty construction caused the death of the owner."

Although no such severe penalty for faulty workmanship exists today, a significant portion of the cost of a row house renovation in large cities is due to tangled building codes. Code compliance can cause time delays measured in months, and the code is subject to interpretation by the inspector assigned to that portion of the city in which the row house renovation is taking place. Generally, the architect includes, by reference, applicable code restrictions in the General Conditions of the specifications, thereby influencing every subsequent section of the contract documents. Most contract documents hold the contractor liable for code-required changes or any additional work not anticipated by the architect. The owner should consult with his lawyer to ascertain his financial responsibility for code-required extras, if any.

In some cities like New York strict fire protection requirements apply when changing a building from one use-classification to another. According to these restrictions, row houses converted for one- and two-family occupancy have to comply with the same expensive fire protection requirements as those applicable to buildings providing accomodations for three or more families.

There are, literally, hundreds of provisions of a code that will directly influence the reconstruction of a row house; most of these will be automatically accounted for by the architect.

WORKING DRAWINGS AND SPECIFICATIONS

When the architectural design satisfies the owner's requirements, the architect — usually after obtaining written approval from the owner — is ready to commence the construction document phase. This consists of preparing working drawings and specifications. Complete working drawings usually include the following items:

1. Complete floor plans at every level, showing location of all partitions.
2. Exterior elevations, if any change is contemplated in the facades.
3. A section through the building, and other sections as required.
4. Interior elevations of all bathrooms and kitchens, showing the extent of tile and cabinet work; also elevations of rooms with special features such as fireplaces, special openings, shelves, etc.
5. Architectural details showing the manner of construction.
6. Structural details.
7. Mechanical drawings showing location of heating and cooling equipment.
8. Electrical plans locating duplex outlets, switches, thermostats, light fixtures, and telephone and television outlets.

This list may be abbreviated for relatively simple renovation projects.

The working drawings graphically indicate all new construction. The more complete they are, the greater the control over construction and the smaller the margin for error. However, since it is practically impossible to thoroughly scrutinize every detail of a building before demolition begins, surprises are not only possible, but should always be expected in renovation work. Beams which originally appeared sound may prove to be unsound when exposed and require replacement; partitions that were thought to be bearing walls may turn out to be nonbearing, etc.

The specifications complement the working drawings; they are a written description of all labor, materials and equipment necessary for the execution and completion of the renovation project. A.I.A. document A-201 (General Conditions of the Contract for Construction) or its equivalent, is included with the specifications. This document outlines the responsibilities of the architect, contractor, and owner and includes instructions regarding the manner of payments to the contractor, the completion of work, the protection of persons and property, changes in the work, and the termination of the contract.

MECHANICAL SYSTEMS

During the construction document phase the mechanical systems must be specified. In the majority of row houses the original heating system generally relied upon a one-pipe steam system with cast-iron radiators. Although durable and easily operated and maintained, this system does not have the versatility and the many advantages of some newer replacements. Furthermore, cast-iron radiators are not particularly ornamental when they intrude into rooms and when recessed in niches they prove less effective than baseboard units which are not particularly adaptable to the one-pipe steam system.

It is for these reasons that the two-pipe hot water system, easily installed at the baseboard level, is preferred today. Its response to calls for heat is much faster than a steam system and when the thermostat is satisfied, and the circulating pump has stopped in the two-pipe hot water system, the heat from the baseboard (or even radiators) diminishes gradually. Loss of heat generated by a one-pipe steam system is much more rapid. For this reason alone, a two-pipe hot water system is usually less expensive to operate and because of its easy adaptability to baseboard installation, proves much less of a decorating problem.

When considering air conditioning, there is another advantage; the hot water system combines well with a cooling unit. Several manufacturers offer through-the-wall units which include both convectors applicable to the hot water system, and the condenser, compressor, and evaporator of the self-contained air conditioning system. The cooling system is operated electrically and offers room-to-room control.

Another heating arrangement is the forced warm air system which circulates warm air through ducts by means of a fan. This system is characterized by its quick response to changing weather demands, and the possibilities it offers for easy, quick summer cooling and winter humidification. The quality of the air introduced into the rooms can also be controlled through filters. Registers and diffusers replace the more ungainly radiators, convectors, and baseboard of other systems, and the need to cut through the facade to install an air conditioning unit is elminated. The disadvantages of this system, however, are its high initial cost, and the difficulty of introducing ducts throughout a house where only minor renovation is required, where detailing may be ruined, or where the vertical ducts would interrupt an intended plan.

The hot water and warm air systems have two features in common: both require a furnace located in the basement, and both are usually controlled by one thermostat — located either in the owner's apartment or outside the building. In contrast, an all-electric building requires no furnace and offers individual room control. Each tenant operates independently with a meter of his own and adjusts the temperature according to his needs, applying for the service individually.

In an electric heating system installation, the basement may be reclaimed for storage, playroom facilities, laundry, workshop, etc., some of which would not be possible if oil- or gas-fired boilers are chosen.

Although electric heat is more efficient than any of the other systems, it also is usually more expensive. In an electrically heated building air conditioning is arranged either by through-the-wall or window units, or by a split-unit system. In this system the compressor and condenser are combined in one unit located in a rear wall or on the roof, and the evaporator and blower are located usually in the space above a bathroom or kitchen. The refrigerant is piped from the condenser to the evaporator through insulated piping, and cool air is distributed through ducts to the various rooms. This system is most effective for floor-through apartments, and can also be adapted to a duplex.

Whichever system is employed, the original cost of heating and cooling equipment and operating costs may be reduced greatly by insulating ceilings and walls. Weatherstripping around windows and doors, together with storm windows, reduce the infiltration of cold air from the outside. Some utilities offer a free survey of the proposed plan, it estimates operating costs, and it may provide a cash rebate incentive for each apartment in an all-electric building, although such sales incentives were more common before the oil crisis.

The foregoing description of heating-cooling systems is necessarily brief; proposed floor plans, the construction budget and many other factors influence the choice of an appropriate system. The building's architect or a consulting engineer is the logical source for additional explanation and suggestions.

PROFESSIONAL AND ARTISTIC ADVICE

During the early phases of renovation planning, as well as during the actual construction, the architect will offer advice and make suggestions to the owner relative to the retention of certain original decorative features or details. He also will assist the owner to select the materials and finishes to be used in the construction including kitchen and bath fixtures. Before the specifications are prepared, however, each of these items is reviewed with the owner for his approval.

At the appropriate time the architect also will prepare and review with the owner all electrical plans. This will confirm the location of all outlets, lighting fixtures, telephone outlets, etc. Since the delivery of lighting fixtures can take an inordinate amount of time, it is advisable that the contractor be instructed to order them as soon as possible to avoid unnecessary delays in construction.

CONSTRUCTION DOCUMENTS

When the construction documents have been completed, they are submitted to various contractors for bidding. It is customary to invite three or more contractors to bid on a row house renovation. Contractors must be informed of any time limit applicable to the construction phase, they must know which contract form will be signed, and they must be acquainted with the amount of time allowed for preparation of the bid as well as the method of submitting the bid.

Usually the contractor is allowed 3 or 4 weeks to prepare his bid for a row house project. During this period he submits the architect's drawings and specifications to various subcontractors to obtain their prices as basis for formulating his over-all bid, which is submitted at an hour and place designated by the architect. The owner should be present at the opening of the bids, at which time he is advised by the architect which contractor should be awarded the contract. The contract invariably is made on a lump sum basis for row house renovation.

When bids from several contractors prove to be approximately the same, it indicates that the working drawings and specifications have been clear and that there has been little need for interpretations or contingency allowances. However, this does not occur too frequently, and highly discrepant bids are not uncommon.

Several factors influence a bid. A union contractor's bid may be higher than one submitted by a nonunion contractor; a general contractor, who does not do his own plumbing and electrical work, may submit a lower bid than one who combines these services. The general availability of work affects a bid, and in particular the amount of work any one of the contractors might have at that moment may alter a bid considerably.

When awarding a contract, it is important to select a firm that is financially sound and reliable, and one that is capable of achieving the required quality of work demanded. Hopefully, the contractor also will be sensitive to the quality of intended construction, for in spite of a careful regard for all contingencies, renovation work invariably reveals surprises or even oversights that require good judgment on the part of the contractor. In most instances row house renovation contracts are awarded to small nonunion builders whose previous work and references must be carefully checked.

CONSTRUCTION PHASE

The construction phase begins once the contract is actually awarded and the building permit obtained. At this point the architect's function is primarily administrative and consists of representing the owner by periodically visiting the site to inspect construction in progress to satisfy himself that it complies with the construction documents. These field trips, however, in no way relieve the contractor of any responsibility.

RELATIONSHIP OF THE ARCHITECT WITH THE CONTRACTOR

As primary arbiter of the contract between owner and contractor, the architect is required to be impartial. When required, the architect will interpret the contract documents to the contractor and furnish him with any required supplementary drawings and details. For changes which the owner may wish to make, the architect will authorize change orders to the contractor. The cost of any such changes should first be obtained from the contractor and then be evaluated by both architect and owner with the latter committing himself to the cost of the changes before they are made. The contractor must submit an application for payment in order to receive each monthly payment. By this means both the owner and the architect are informed of the percentage of work already completed and the amount due for each trade, according to the contractor's original estimate. Before granting approval by issuing a certificate for payment to the contractor, it is the duty of the architect to compare the application with his own observation of work performed. Normally, 10% of the application for payment is retained by the owner each month to protect his interest and assure corrective work if and when necessary. Upon "substantial completion of the work," a term usually defined in the construction contract, the architect will advise that the owner pay the contractor the 10% previously withheld. Usually, the owner and the architect will have prepared a check list, or "punch list," as it is called, indicating the work remaining to be done.

During the construction phase the building department assigns an inspector to the project. It is his responsibility to see that the finished design conforms to the plans filed with the department. In this supervisory role he will enforce the appropriate standards for each phase of construction and may withhold approval until he is satisfied that these standards have been met. When the project has been completed, and the inspector is satisfied that the pertinent codes and regulations have been observed, a Certificate of Occupancy is issued.

Depending upon the size and complexity of the renovation, the process that commences with the selection of an architect and ends with the issuance of a Certificate of Occupancy may take from 6 months to a year and one half. When a row house is *completely* renovated, an owner should plan on 6 months for the architect's work and bidding and 6 or more additional months for the construction work.

In any renovation an architect's advice, his planning, and his design are the deciding factors in whether or not the reconstruction is a success or a failure. For these reasons it is imperative that the owner choose wisely and select an architect who fully understands his needs and is capable of expressing his wishes.

Chapter 11
Row House Interior Design

With limited footage in the front and back of the building the essence of row house design depends almost entirely upon the development of interior architecture. Whether this planning is done by an architect, or by an architect and interior designer, or an owner, the success of the project often stands or falls on the skillful manipulation of these internal spaces. Working with the basic character of the structure, the interior designer develops an ambiance which reflects the personality of the client. Consequently, close cooperation between client, architect, interior designer, and builder is imperative.

Where does interior design begin and architecture end? Is an interior designer required? In actuality the two disciplines are integrally interwoven. With the architect and the interior designer coordinating their efforts, the creative result will exceed what each could have done independently. At no added expense to the client the completed project will have a clarity of design and unification of approach, with each specialist, expert in his field, contributing to an integrated and visually cohesive building. Rapport between architect and interior designer is essential with the former responsible for the structural and mechanical design, and the latter responsible for the finishing and furnishing of the project. Selection of an interior designer, therefore, is an important decision. No one knows the family life style more intimately than the physician and the interior designer, and deciding who will translate personality into a living environment is a combination of recommendation and exposure. Shelter magazines purposely cover a variety of tastes, and when a particular photograph captures attention the row house owner should note the name of the interior designer.

There are several organizations of interior designers: American Institute of Interior Designers, National Society of Interior Designers, and the American Institute of Industrial Designers, and membership in these organizations insures a degree of competance. Many industrial designers are highly qualified to do residential interiors. If the client is receptive, and has a realistic budget, the industrial designer may be just the professional to bring fresh ideas and a new approach to a row house. No matter who is chosen the client must investigate professional training and inspect previous work.

All professionals offer the same service: time and talent. The contractual bases of working are variations of payment for hours expended on the work. Three basic methods of compensation are: design fee, percentage over cost, and retail price. The design fee may be a lump sum amount or time charges, paid for the total job, with all purchases charged at wholesale costs. Many interior designers' fees are a percentage over the wholesale cost, resulting in a combination of design fee plus percentage over costs. The percentage charged over wholesale cost will determine whether initial design and drafting services are billed separately. Interior designers often bill a preliminary design fee which may be applied against future purchases. Since residential furniture and fabrics are priced at retail, interior designers may charge their clients this price on all purchases. Some professionals charge an additional design fee over retail prices.

Designers act as agents for their clients. Therefore, the usual sequence of payments begins with a deposit against any purchase, with the balance due either before or upon delivery. Since the interior designer is acting as the client's representative, there are no returns. Thus it is imperative that the client be thoroughly familiar with what has been ordered before approving the purchase.

The special character of the row house offers one of the most interesting and exciting design challenges. The personality of the house may be established by the very character of the block. Before entering the front door there is an awareness of a special consistency of design and scale, and in a sensitive renovation there is respect for original architectural features. Whether the building interior is modern or traditional, the appropriateness of the materials and details must be maintained in the exterior renovation. Aluminum entrance doors and fluorescent lights negate the basic character of the building, while a careful selection of color and texture of entrance materials, combined with the warmth of incandescent light, can set the mood for an entire building.

Most row houses have high ceilings and with a 10- to 12-foot ceiling a 3-foot wide corridor can appear magnificent, and what other building type can boast of a hallway where a hanging fixture over 4 feet long is effective? Wallcovering can have a pattern with a large repeating design to strengthen this sense of the vertical. Fortunately the old master craftsmen used paneling and handrail details at eye level and below, with gracious cornices at the ceiling to top off the space. They assumed that in between the architectural details the individual owner would select pattern and color. In a row house renovation changes must be made, and the secret of a sensitive renovation is making changes which do not conflict with the basic character of the building. For example, in a 10-foot high hall a 6-foot 8-inch high entrance door appears entirely out of scale; the space above the door must also be a design element. By forming an "overdoor," with a simple jamb trim to 9 feet, and a swath of color over both, or by using an 8-foot

A row house in good restorable condition can compete with the best period architecture when redone. (Photo © 1979 by Jim Kalett)

high door at every entrance, the sense of original scale can be maintained. Wall sconces can lower the height of the lighting to a point where it is needed and serve as interesting visual interruptions to an otherwise dull wall. In their original state many row houses have salvageable carvings and mirrors. These may be reused to break the monotony of hallways. Wall-mounted art may be lighted by swivel spots in the ceiling, which serve as a source of light for an entire area. At no extra cost, color can add variety to each floor or stairway landing. Although a major initial expense, carpeting the stairs and corridors of a row house is practically mandatory: the sound from traffic on stairs can be muffled only by carpeting. Through judicious selection of the carpet fiber, maintenance problems can be minimized.

The most demanding design problem of a row house is the interior space between the front and back rooms. Whether the building is to consist of half-floor rental units, floor-through apartments, or duplex apartments, the problems are similar. The interior areas are the transition spaces, and frequently bathrooms, kitchens and dressing rooms are located in this area. In the transition spaces the architect and interior designer, working together, can develop a sense of scale which enhances the visual impact of the major rooms. A hung ceiling can make a standard bath and kitchen acceptable; it not only provides storage space above, but creates a change of scale through proportion of height to width. Variations in ceiling height produce a sense of drama which may be appreciated when entering larger adjacent rooms. When a row house is to be used as a private residence, an impression of the total house begins at the front door, and the initial visual impression established the visitor's overall esthetic response to the entire building.

Row houses are especially successful nighttime spaces; they were originally designed for candlelight and gaslight. As a consequence, preplanned lighting is essential, with color actively affecting lighting decisions. Deeper wall and floor tones demand more lighting, and recessed lighting and hanging fixtures should be considered when establishing the general atmosphere of an entire area.

All main living areas must be planned in advance. Components of the space should be designed to scale, indicating all intended furniture. Each piece must be drawn on a furniture plan, and wall elevations must be considered so that furniture may be related to the vertical proportions of the room. Often furniture which appears large in a normal apartment may be totally out of scale in a row house. When complete, the furniture plan elevations and the architectural and mechanical plans are ready to be coordinated. With the furniture designed to scale, the lighting plan can be developed to fit the requirements of the layout, with electric, telephone, television and hi-fi outlets verified. Such careful planning also will prevent supply and return air ducts from being blocked, and air conditioning can be planned to provide draft-free ventilation.

At this design stage built-in furniture requirements can be decided, and room sizes may be adjusted to accommodate furnishings. Children's rooms,

Occasionally a relic of the past will turn up and be appropriate for the finished building. (Photo © 1979 by Jim Kalett)

in particular, must be carefully designed in advance, since in a row house these areas often are smaller than their suburban counterparts and it is essential to maximize the floor space in these rooms.

With careful furniture planning, imaginative, nonrectilinear design may be achieved if desired, but this requires careful programming of the occupant's needs and usage as well as a regard for special limitations. For instance, a break in a wall may be suitable for a built-in desk-dresser combination, thus freeing valuable wall space for other use. The master bedroom can double as a study or library if the sleeping area is separated; or folding partitions which allow for both privacy and spaciousness may be introduced. In an existing row house room dimensions often are overgenerous for their intended use, so with creative architecture and interior design a multipurpose plan can be evolved.

The client's decision regarding colors and textures should be made simultaneously with construction drawings. Exposed brick is a fundamental tool of row house renovations, and where these walls can be best used and whether they will be left natural or painted evolves from early interior design decisions confirmed by inspection after demolition. After planning the layout and coordinating colors, decisions about materials, textures and patterns become simplified.

Chapter 12
Row House Financing

Most individuals contemplating the purchase of real estate are compelled to turn to banks or other lending institutions for financial backing of their project in the form of a mortgage.

For a renovation, before discussing a possible loan with any type of lender, the owner must know what amount of money will be needed to finance the purchase and reconstruction of the row house. A rule of thumb determination is: four to five times the annual gross rents expected after completion of the renovation (including a rental value applied to the owner's apartment, if any) will approximate the level of mortgage that can be secured. A far better approach is to engage a real estate appraiser or other professional whose survey and estimate of the mortgage required is more reliable, even though he must be paid a fee.

Some row house buyers feel quite competent in handling the mortgage negotiations by themselves, thereby avoiding brokerage fees; others believe that procuring a mortgage is too complicated a procedure for them and consequently rely upon a mortgage broker to solve the problems related to obtaining such a loan.

MORTGAGES NEGOTIATED BY INDIVIDUAL OWNERS

To save the expense of mortgage brokerage fees, some owners prefer to negotiate with a lending agency by themselves. During a prosperous mortgage market when the supply of funds exceeds demand, there is not too much difficulty in obtaining a loan in this way since loan officers are inclined to welcome all comers. However, when the supply of available funds is low, opportunities open to the owner are markedly fewer, and the list of banks specializing in row house renovations is narrowed. In addition, the obtaining of a row house mortgage has always been handicapped by a peculiarity of the loan market: for some unaccountable reason, banks in the immediate neighborhood of the building being renovated often are not particularly interested in lending their funds for such projects. It is much more probable that the individual seeking a loan will be more successful in other parts of the city, or even elsewhere in the state. For the loan negotiator, then, this adds still another problem, for he can hardly expect to be familiar with all lenders throughout the city, let alone throughout the state. There are cases on record where owners were forced to carry a vacant building for 2 years, while time was spent searching fruitlessly for a mortgage.

MORTGAGE BROKER

If for no other reason than the fact that the average mortgage broker is well equipped to contact such widespread sources of funds, a mortgage broker often is required.

The average mortgage broker's fee for services is 1-1/2 to 2% of the face amount of the mortgage, and this fee is paid at the time when the mortgage is closed. If the financing package arranged for the building consists of a building or construction loan, and a permanent mortgage, the broker's fee is paid at the time of the "first Advance" of construction mortgage funds.

The broker obtains one commitment from a lender (usually a bank) either for the construction mortgage, the permanent mortgage, or a combination of the two. If the face amounts of the loans are similar, and if they are arranged simultaneously, the broker will receive the same fee for all three transactions. However, if the construction loan is arranged prior to and separate from the permanent loan, two commissions are usually payable.

Many mortgages which brokers negotiate are placed with banks outside the local area; generally such mortgages are serviced by correspondents located near the property. These correspondents act as agents, and since they have the assistance of an accounting department, a legal department, and an appraisal department, all paperwork requisite to a loan is prepared by them. The lender, wherever he may be located, lends on the correspondent's recommendations, together with an outside confirming appraisal prepared by an independent appraiser. In such instances all charges for services rendered are paid by the borrower.

In addition to the mortgage broker's fees and his own lawyer's fees, the owner of a row house also can expect to be responsible for the following charges, all paid in advance, or on the initial "closing" of the mortgage:

Approximate Costs
Based Upon a $100,000 Building Loan
And Permanent Mortgage

	Low	Average	High
Bank's lawyer's fee	250	500	$700
Bank's appraisal	0	200	400
Outside confirming appraisal	200	300	400
Credit report cost	20	25	40
Title insurance	400	400	400

Some states have a mortgage or conveyance tax at ¼ of 1% to 1% of the mortgage.

TITLE INSURANCE

Title insurance, as the name implies, assures the buyer that title to the building is free and clear of all prior encumbrances, and it is required by most lenders. Title insurance covers such risks and future discoveries as: forgery, a missing spouse, a missing heir, unpaid taxes, improper documents, unpaid unreleased liens, a broken chain of title, federal tax liens, and recorded judgments. Usually the title insurance company of record assumes that the building previously had title insurance, and under such conditions all that is necessary is to update the previous search, rather than undertake a new and exhaustive title search.

Competition between title companies is keen, and it is advisable that the buyer of a row house consult with his lawyer so that he may be guided accordingly. The lawyer may suggest an abstract firm, which operates in the guise of a middleman between owner and title company and generally, abstract companies offer faster service.

LENDER FEES

A mortgage applicant often may become bewildered and confused by the casual references to: bonuses, points, fees, discounts, service charges, etc., without realizing that all of these terms actually mean nothing more than a fee which the lender may expect in addition to whatever interest rate has been agreed upon. This fee is a one-time charge and is usually deducted from the mortgage proceeds. For example, in the instance of a $100,000 construction loan and permanent mortgage, the bank may require a 2% building loan fee, or $2000 in addition to a $1-, $2-, $3-, or $4000 additional fee as a bonus to induce a bank to make the loan. Thus, a building loan fee of 2% and a bonus of 4% amounts to 6% (or $6000 on a $100,000 loan commitment).

Under the circumstances above, the borrower commits himself to repay $100,000 to the bank over the term of the loan, but he *receives* only $94,000 in cash. However, the interest rate agreed upon is applied to the full $100,000.

The percentage level of these points, or bonuses, generally works inversely with the interest rate: the higher the interest, the lower the points, or bonus. As an example of the current mortgage scene, one institution charges 9% on row house construction mortgages for 1 year, but also charges a 2% (one-time) fee. Thus the effective interest rate over the term of the loan is higher than 9%. The average current effective yield for a construction loan of this type today is between 10 and 30%, considering both interest and bonus or fee. Should interest rates ease, the combined rate could drop to a possible 9%.

SUBORDINATION

Of all the specialized real estate terminology that must be learned by row house buyers, one of the most important is "subordination". A lending institution, such as a bank, is required by law to limit its loans to those in a *first loan* or *primary loan* position, in spite of the fact that the building could have as many as four mortgage loans outstanding against it. Thus the bank's first mortgage represents a *primary* lien against a building.

If for instance an owner buys a mortgage-free building with the seller accepting a "purchase-money mortgage" as an aid to the sale, that mortgage automatically would be in the *primary* position. However, no bank is permitted to hold a construction or permanent mortgage which is in a *secondary* (or subordinate) position. Therefore, in order to comply with this legal requirement, the seller should be in a position to offer his own concession by subordinating his purchase money mortgage to a construction loan when the latter is placed on the building later. In brief, subordination occurs when the holder of a mortgage permits another mortgage to be placed ahead of his own.

The situation is further complicated when a first mortgage already exists and the seller agrees to a purchase-money second mortgage as an aid to the sale. Under these conditions, in order for the bank to provide construction financing, the seller's second mortgage necessarily would move (subordinate) to the third position, the first mortgage would move (subordinate) to the second position, leaving the bank in its mandatory first position. On the other hand if the first mortgage has no clause permitting subordination it must be paid in full with the new order of mortgages being: the seller holds the subordinated second, and the bank holds the new first mortgage. Undoubtedly, many banks holding row house mortgages that are 10 or more years old would welcome having such mortgages paid, primarily because of their low interest rates. Subordination in such cases offers very few problems.

Arranging new construction financing for a building often means that a low interest mortgage must be paid in full, and many of these mortgages carry prepayment penalties designed to compensate the lender for premature repayment. Thus a fixed dollar amount or percentage penalty may have to be paid in addition to the face amount of the remaining mortgage. Consequently, when taking title to a building, the owner should investigate whether or not any prepayment penalties are to be found in the existing financing documents.

To explain subordination more fully consider the following example:

Purchase price of unrenovated building	$100,000
Cash required	50,000
Existing first mortgage	25,000
Seller accepts second, or purchase money, subordinated mortgage	25,000

In this hypothetical situation after the plans have been drawn, the owner will ask a lender for a construction and permanent mortgage. After demolition and rough carpentry the bank advances a sum of $35,000, $25,000 of which is used to pay off the existing first mortgage, leaving $10,000 for the first payment to the contractor. This is known as a simultaneous closing, after which the bank then holds the new first mortgage, and the second mortgage remains in the second position.

This is the essence of subordination and demonstrates how important it is for the buyer of a row house to have a dependable and well-informed lawyer to negotiate the necessary terms of purchase including, if possible, a subordinated mortgage. Likewise the choice of correct terminology is particularly important, since subordination can be mishandled through an improperly drawn agreement. If in the example cited above subordination had not been obtained, *both* mortgagees would have had to be satisfied (i.e. repaid) before a construction mortgage could have been placed on the property.

When mortgage terminology is misleading or sufficiently unclear to cause a disagreement over subordination, the owner is in a position to sue for subordination. However, when this happens, work at the construction site ceases, and vandalism can become a major problem. Also monthly costs continue to mount and an outstanding mortgage commitment may be forfeited because of time expiration. When absolutely unavoidable, an additional fee may be offered as an incentive for subordination, or another choice is to pay off the mortgage and rearrange the building's financing.

Subordination and the Seller

Subordination does benefit the seller, but only to a limited extent. For instance, in most markets top prices are being demanded by sellers, and subordination certainly is an aid to selling property in such a market. Subordination also supports the seller's price demands so that he is not forced into a position of compromising by lowering his price in order to make a sale. Since many prospective buyers would not be able to accumulate sufficient funds for a row house project were it not for the potential of subordination, there is no limiting the marketability of the building, as there might be otherwise.

When a seller refuses to consider subordination, a second mortgage construction loan may serve as an alternative. Such loans are expensive, carrying 8 to 10% interest as the funds are advanced, in addition to a 10% discount. As a result, the annual rate for such financing would amount to approximately 20%. But since the loan is "drawn down" during a maximum period of about a year, the actual interest paid is lower. In New York state the statutory maximum limit on the interest rate charged is 24% when the loan is made to a corporation, thus with current high interest rates, very few conventional loans are made to individuals or partnerships since 7½% is the statutory maximum rate that can be charged to these forms of ownership.

CONSTRUCTION LOAN PAYMENTS

Once proper financing has been arranged and a contractor engaged, advances are made to the owner in accordance with the mortgage commitment schedule of payments, and in turn these payments are made to the contractor by the owner.

The average row house reconstruction involves six or seven advances of funds, and an inspection by the lender is usually made prior to each advance. The advances generally occur as follows:

Advance number	Occurs upon completion of:	And this percent of the Total loan is paid (less a percentage withheld until completion)
1	Demolition, rough carpentry	30%
2	Rough plumbing, rough wiring	20%
3	Tubs in, plus brown/scratch coat plaster, or sheetrock up	15%
4	White plaster or taping and spackling sheetrock	10%
5	Floors and bath tile, kitchen cabinets, etc.	10%
6	Hanging fixtures, kitchen appliances, hardware, etc.	10%
7	Painting, carpet, if any, etc.	5%

The final payment is usually preceded by the issuance of a permanent Certificate of Occupancy at which time the rent of a certain number of units may have to be guaranteed by the owner. In practice 5 to 10% of the total commitment is withheld until absolutely all items on the completion list (or "punch list") have been attended to. Sometimes these items can be as minor as: "Paint second coat on door jamb on third floor hall door": however, they must be completed before the withheld 5 to 10% is paid.

To obtain a mortgage commitment the owner sometimes must post a 2% "good faith" deposit with the lender. If the mortgage is not closed within 2 or 3 months as specified by the lender, the lender has the right to cancel the commitment and retain the deposit, or the lender may extend the commitment and adjust its interest rate.

CONDOMINIUM FINANCING

In general, banks in many cities have never taken the trouble to study this particular type of ownership in detail when applied to small projects such as row house renovation, and they neither fully understand all of the ramifications of condominiums, nor are they inclined to make such mortgage arrangements. Additionally, this type of mortgage would be extremely expensive; for example, when financing a five-unit building, the bank would be compelled to make five separate loans, with five sets of legal fees, etc. Apparently from the banks' point of view, this repetitive procedure is more trouble than it is worth for small projects especially during periods when money is tight. The situation is improving slowly in many cities, however.

COOPERATIVE FINANCING

Banks are beginning to recognize the fact that the cooperative is considered as a necessary, emerging vehicle of ownership. Much progress has been made during the past few years to educate lenders as far as the mechanics of cooperatives are concerned, emphasizing the ultimate value to the lender, the borrower, and the community as well.

The general practice of cooperative mortgaging is as follows. The recorded owner of a row house mortgage is usually designated as a "dummy" corporation with no other assets than the building itself. In addition to a mortgage, however, the lender may insist that one (or more) of the individuals in the cooperative sign a note. In the event of complications, this arrangement provides the bank with means of legally prosecuting the note first, rather than immediately foreclosing the mortgage. Suing on a note may take considerable time and a default is usually pursued promptly. Immediate foreclosure is preferred because the value of the premises can be predetermined, but the extent of personal assets of the signee is a matter of conjecture. The reader can be assured that the bank will be sufficiently protected when the mortgage is placed.

LIENS

Liens are charges recorded against the title of a building. As a rule, liens arise from unpaid subcontractor's bills and are most effective when recorded before the permanent mortgage closing occurs since they automatically cloud the title to a building. To by-pass the title complication and to permit the owner to obtain his mortgage closing, the owner may bond the lien. Unfortunately, some bank attorneys refuse to accept lien bonding, in which case the owner is compelled to pay the disputed bill before completing his financing. However, most contractors' bills are usually settled before any drastic measures are taken by either side.

Chapter 13
Standard Row House Existing Construction

The structure of a row house is extremely simple, direct, and relatively uncomplicated. For masonry buildings, front and rear walls, although tied into the party walls on either side, are self-supporting. The brick party walls, 12 or 16 inches thick, support rows of wooden joists, usually 3" x 10"s at 16 inches on center at each floor. These in turn support a subfloor and partitions framed with 2" x 4" or 3" x 4" studs. Openings in the floors require that joists be doubled at either side of the opening, with the intermediate joists supported by headers. Above the subfloor is a finish floor, usually of oak or maple, but occasionally of softwood on the upper floors. The party walls and partitions are of plaster and lath on 2" x 4" stud construction. There is tile in the bathrooms, wainscoting in halls on the first and often second floors, and generally some marble in the vestibule. Marble often was employed to fashion the more elegant intricately carved fireplaces. In wood frame construction the exterior is usually clapboards, shingles, or composition material, but the party walls are almost always brick.

Current renovation operations differ in practically no way from former decades, and the materials and construction methods are practically the same; only the very high quality of workmanship and specialized, artistic skills have disappeared. The former profusion of decorative detail has been replaced by plain surfaces; where formerly there was a parquet floor with an elaborate border, now there is strip flooring. Because of its lower cost, plasterboard frequently replaces plaster, and wainscoting and moldings have practically disappeared. To conserve space, bathrooms and kitchens have been reduced in size and less tile is being used. Practically all of these up-to-date architectural effects, features, and materials can be justified on the basis of high costs to replace existing materials.

Ingenuity can be used in preserving or reusing as many of the old and beautiful features of a row house as possible, often employing them in an entirely new context. As an example, wainscoting taken from one wall may be used again in an entirely different manner in another room, perhaps on the ceiling, but such reuse generally carries a high labor cost. Fine old

Window treatments are part of the interior design; many row houses were built with window shutters like these. (Photo © 1979 by Jim Kalett)

doors may be used in place of ordinary cabinet work as counter fronts in the living room or kitchen, and beautiful wooden mantels can be reworked as decorative frames for newly constructed fireplaces. Modern architecture does not reject this type of detail, it merely employs it in an entirely different manner, dictated by current work practices and natural economic restraints. Where interest was formerly achieved by treating a wall as a surface to be decorated, today these same surfaces are considered as a form to be sculpted.

Chapter 14
The Contractor

A contractor is essentially a manager of materials, money, men and time, and if any one of these four parts of the equation is slighted, the construction result will not be satisfactory.

Since there are bound to be endless problems associated with the task of translating the architect's plans into three-dimensional form, and the contractor is the person who holds the key to all these problems, it is of paramount importance for the owner to select a contractor in whom he may have complete confidence. The contractor must prove himself competent from the start, for once renovation has begun, changing firms can prove extremely expensive to the owner in both time and money. And litigation with a contractor with the need for bills, receipts, claims for extras, counter claims, etc., has to be one of the least productive legal areas involving a homeowner. The reader may know of many owner-contractor relationships which deteriorated, and few or none where there was no disagreement. But there are ways to reduce the likelihood of disagreement.

CHOOSING A CONTRACTOR

There are a number of ways by which a contractor may be selected, and many factors to consider in making the choice. Some of the more important are:

1. Recommendations made by the owner's architect, usually as a result of his prior experience with the contractor.
2. Recommendations of other architects who have been associated with the contractor on other construction projects.
3. The owner's personal inspection of buildings constructed or renovated by the proposed contractor.
4. Conversations with previous clients of the proposed firm.
5. Suggestions made by municipal agencies.
6. Firms presently operating in the immediate geographic area of the proposed renovation who can be identified by noting signs that appear on nearby renovations while in progress.

7. Suggestions of friends undertaking similar renovation projects.
8. Noting the contractor whose name is mentioned in published articles about row house renovation, etc.
9. The response to such questions as financial responsibility — questions that should be answered satisfactorily by the bidder prior to the award of the contract or the start of construction.

CONTRACTOR AND OWNER RELATIONSHIP

Even the most ideal relationship between owner and contractor can be marked by differences and misunderstanding, but if the owner has chosen a competent contractor, these problems can be quickly resolved. Many contractor-owner conflicts which ultimately become serious can be traced to an unwillingness of one party to understand the position of the other. These situations often center around extra charges and to avoid such problems an owner may eventually agree to omit one item in favor of another, thereby avoiding an unnecessary dispute.

When a need for changes arises, the owner should thoroughly discuss the proposed changes with the contractor to avoid any possibility of misunderstanding, and prepare a detailed written list, together with an agreement as to the amount of additional cost, or credit, which is signed by both parties.

Obviously the best advice for the owner interested in avoiding difficulties with his contractor is to spend sufficient time with his architect in an effort to anticipate *all* changes and inclusions, thereby reaching the almost unobtainable goal of no changes occurring after construction begins. Then, while all structural defects or changes may remain unknown until the demolition is completed, the job can be bid in two phases: the demolition section, separate from the balance of reconstruction, and the latter, rebid, upon the exposure of the building's interior. This policy should hold job-produced changes to an absolute minimum, although complicating the bidding procedure and delaying completion and occupancy.

One source of contractor-owner irritation may arise when the owner discusses a change with one of the workmen on the job, or worse, instructs the workman to make a change. The owner must realize that all changes, even constructive criticism, must be directed to the contractor, his supervisor, or the foreman on the job. Either one of the latter two individuals is usually at the site at all times and has been instructed by his employer how to handle change requests originated by the owner. Work should not progress while any problem of major proportions — or any disagreement about extras — remains unresolved.

Finish work and cabinet work represent two of the most frequent areas of contractor-owner disagreement, and these are the areas in which it is the most difficult for the architect to write a tight specification. Furthermore, when the job is completed, they are open to the widest range of interpretation as to whether or not the work of the contractor is satisfactory, and if it has followed the specifications. The skilled craftsmen of former years are not available today, and the owner cannot expect that caliber of high-grade work. The best insurance for the owner is to inspect several projects completed by the contractor to see whether or not the finish work on these jobs is satisfactory. Poor plastering, sheetrock taping, and painting will appear here, and the owner can at least see the probable level of quality he may expect in his own building. Checking with the department of buildings, or with the building inspector assigned to the immediate geographic area, may indicate instances of poor quality on the part of the contractor under consideration.

Differences of opinion often occur between contractor and architect, primarily because each individual considers the project from a different point of view. To avoid the possibility of misunderstandings, the wise owner will select an architect who has had previous experience in row house renovation work, and will award the construction to a contractor well acquainted with row house work. This will provide much better results for it insures that disagreements will probably not be related to unfamiliarity with the type of work being done.

RENOVATION AND THE CHOICE OF CONTRACTOR

In a "commercial" renovation project (i.e. usually one containing many small units) the prudent owner chooses a contractor whose principal asset is speed of completion coupled with reasonable quality. Such a project is usually undertaken according to plans that are simple and explicit, with few or no changes requested by the owner, and most repetitive construction items (such as standard size doors and windows) require little special consideration. Assuming that the average architect-designed row house renovation requires 6 to 8 months for completion, a "commercial" project will save about 2 months of valuable time. Contractors who are experienced in custom work will function poorly when employed to do commercial work, and the opposite is certainly true.

Since this difference in approach due to quality may not be apparent when receiving bids from contractors, it is the obligation of the owner or architect to thoroughly investigate completed buildings before deciding upon a certain individual or firm.

HOW THE CONTRACTOR IS MOBILIZED

The average construction firm engaging in row house renovation usually specializes in either carpentry or masonry work. Of all the trades required for successful completion of such a project, these two represent the largest single portion of the contract. Thus the average contractor assumes full responsibility for either or both of these two areas and subcontracts for the balance of the work. There are some contracting firms, however, which do most of the work themselves and subcontract only the electrical, heating, and plumbing trades.

BIDDING PROCEDURE FROM THE CONTRACTOR'S VIEWPOINT

Unless there are special details or unusual products involved in a proposed renovation, the time required for a contractor to prepare a bid can be measured in days rather than weeks. In addition, many contractors do not even visit the building during the preparation of their bids. This is especially true when the plans call for complete interior demolition and if the contractor has had previous experience with buildings built about the same time so he can foretell what will be encountered. Bids prepared by contractors for row house renovation are usually "padded" somewhat to provide for any problems that may be uncovered when the interior demolition has been completed.

An exception to the above may be termed the "structural unknown," such as how many floor joists or beams may have to be replaced either through inspection by the architect or as required by the building inspector. The experienced architect provides for an allowance in the bid for such replacements, and the contractor might profit by visiting the building prior to preparing his bid to see if there is extensive remedial work to be done on the exterior other than normal pointing of masonry, cleaning, or painting.

THE ROLE OF THE BUILDING INSPECTOR

One intangible throughout the construction process over which neither the architect, owner, nor contractor have any control are changes or additions required by the inspector on the project. If a required change seems unrealistic to both the architect and the contractor, there usually is a well-defined appeal procedure available to the owner. Should the possibility of an appeal arise, the architect can advise what steps should be taken. Although it occurs infrequently, a midjob change of inspectors can disrupt construction and cause additional work. Obviously there is no way to plan for this contingency.

The construction inspector, as distinguished from the inspectors for other trades, if the municipality has such other inspectors, has the final authority relative to approval of the work. When he "signs off the job," he is stating that all work has been performed satisfactorily and according to the applicable building code. Most inspectors look for reasonable work

A close-up view of the facade details of a limestone row house reveals the high quality of work of nineteenth-century craftsmen.

in compliance with the code, but some larger cities have unscrupulous individuals, and if a "pay-off" is requested, the owner's architect or attorney should be consulted.

OWNER'S WORK IN THE BUILDING

There never should be any objections on the part of the average contractor concerning the owner's right of access to the building during construction. This permission is usually granted as long as the owner's presence does not interfere with the contractor's progress, particularly during the day. The owner himself may wish to do some work such as: repair and replace leaded glass windows, construct bookcases, strip paint, or refinish such items as moldings, trim, doors, etc. In addition, the owner may wish to have other tradesmen visit the building for work not included in the contract, such as awning installation, shades, drapery hardware, security devices, etc. The owner should be cautioned, however, not to tamper with or alter work completed by the contractor. As suggested earlier, any changes should be discussed with the contractor in person.

TIME REQUIRED FOR COMPLETION

The most rapid type of renovation is usually classified as a "commercial" project, in contrast to an architect-designed, or custom, renovation. This type of renovation, even when ten dwelling units are planned, should take no more than 5 to 6 months to complete. A building divided into floor-through apartments, with one or more floors reserved for owner occupancy, will require more time: 6 to 8 months should be allowed. Construction delays are often caused by changes; therefore, the fewer changes, the more certain is the contractor to complete the project on time.

One of the longest apparent delays encountered in construction is during the plastering stage. This is mainly because plasterers can work only when all other workmen are out of the building. Another source of delay is when a building is being renovated with FHA guaranteed or other special financing, if only because an inspector for the lender must approve the work as it progresses. Often, all changes must be lender-approved, and obtaining this approval can easily cause a week's delay each time approval is required.

Some types of construction are more affected and influenced by poor weather than are row house renovation projects. The only exception to this would occur if there were no heat in the building during extremely cold weather. As a general rule, the old boiler is usually removed early in the demolition process, and the new one is not installed until nearly the end of the project. Thus work in an unheated building will proceed much more slowly than at any other season, since when it is too cold, concrete cannot be poured, tile laid, nor can masonry work or plastering be undertaken, and the efficiency of other tradesmen is reduced.

GUARANTEES

The normal guarantee that can be expected from a contractor is for one year, and this covers workmanship and materials as well as leaks, negligent installations, etc. In addition, the contractor usually passes on to the owner any warranties that he receives which cover manufactured equipment (such as water heaters, kitchen appliances, air conditioners, etc.).

Chapter 15
Building Costs

This chapter is not intended to be a treatise on the computation of building costs, nor does it thoroughly cover the subject of row house renovation costs — much more space would be necessary to do justice to such a subject. It is intended to be a primer for the novice, presenting some important guidelines to illustrate how renovation costs are determined, some of the factors that influence those costs, and how the cost of a proposed renovation can be approximated. However, before considering renovation costs specifically, some background of the general building cost climate must be considered.

BUILDING COSTS — RECENT HISTORY

The last time the cost-to-build ever went *down* was in 1949; since then an upward trend began and has continued to the present. From 1951 to 1967 average increases approximated 2½% annually and increases were as much as 12% annually from 1968 to the mid-1970's. Since then there appears to be no end in sight for erratic surges of an 8 to 12% annual increase in construction costs.

To complicate the cost problem, contractors are not bidding as competitively as in prior years, thus in-the-bid allowances for profit and overhead are higher. The obvious conclusion for the prospective buyer is that he must measure costs on a day-to-day basis with the possibility that any major interruption in construction or renovation may significantly affect bids. This could cause a spread between preliminary estimates and the low bid, if costs rise, and possibly lead to a deterioration of the architect-client relationship, for it will appear that the architect's original estimate was too low.

The outlook for increases in the cost-to-build may be summarized as: 4 to 12% per year for the next several years, unless there is a marked downswing in the economy. And even this rule-of-thumb must be interpreted according to the peculiarities of the project. To demonstrate the wide divergence in price of renovations, two different cases may be cited.

One of New York City's least expensive row house renovations was accomplished a few years ago in Brooklyn. The building, having been occupied by a single family since its construction in the late 1800's, was in remarkably good condition. All that was required was some plaster to be patched and painted, and a good, thorough top-to-bottom cleaning — entire cost, $500.00. This plus a $3500 new kitchen cost the new owner-occupant $4,000 for renovation.

One of New York's most expensive brownstones was located on Manhattan's East Side. It was described to the writer by a banker being asked for a mortgage, as follows: "A corporation president bought the building for $400,000 and invested $275,000 in the renovation, and basically the only two significant features of the renovation were a marble foyer and central air conditioning."

Somewhere between these two extremes lies the "normal" row house renovation cost.

The condition of urban buildings slated for either public or private rehabilitation varies from prime (where finishes, details, and mechanical systems are complete and require little or no repair) to extremely poor (where finishes have been destroyed or are missing, mechanical systems inoperative or destroyed, possible damage from water leaks, missing windows, etc.). The rehabilitation of an older building in prime condition may be superficial and the cost low, with new bathrooms or new kitchens the only required items. This type of rehabilitation will interest those who wish to return the building near to its original condition, often for single family occupancy. However, most rehabilitations involve complete demolition and removal of partitions, finishes, plumbing, heating, and electrical systems. In many instances, the subfloor and floor joists are retained, together with the public stairs, but dependent upon their condition and pertinent provision of the building code.

SPECIFIC FACTORS INFLUENCING CONSTRUCTION COSTS

1. Range of Bids

One major difference between rehabilitation and new construction is in the spread between high and low bids. As an example, bids for a "quality" job, a large five-unit air conditioned building, were as follows: $109,000, $130,000, $150,000, $170,000, and $180,000. These bids assumed retention of the building's shell, some windows, roof and subfloors, stairs, and fireplaces; everything else was to be new.

While the low bidder was not qualified and the high bidder provided the courtesy bid, nevertheless the remaining three produced a 30% spread between low and high. Ultimately, the $130,000 bid was negotiated down to $105,000, and construction went forward to successful completion.

The $105,000 bid was still $10,000 above the sum budgeted for the work, a situation which many owners face.

2. Contractor Differences and Competency

A simple fact to be realized from the start is that just as individual contractors differ, their personal attitude toward estimating differs. While certain contractors maintain a somewhat standardized approach to estimating even these individuals may raise or lower their bids when the need seems to arise. What may be a "justifiable" margin of profit to one may be modified by another, merely to have his bid accepted.

When renovation is undertaken by a small contractor, there are other complications that can arise. The owner may suddenly discover that his contractor has overextended himself, even though demands of the particular job are limited. A further problem is that the contractor may not be familiar with valuable new products or techniques necessary for successful completion of that particular project. The contractor may have limited working capital or substantial employee turn-over, resulting in his workers performing at lower levels of efficiency. In addition, the contractor or his employees may occasionally misinterpret the plans or specifications, calling for time-consuming remedial work.

3. Inability of the Contractor to Estimate Properly

Many contractors involved in rehabilitation work cannot afford the overhead of an office staff; they act as their own estimators, and for many small contractors actual cost records may be unavailable or unreliable; without them, estimates will be less accurate and probably higher due to a greater allowance for the unknown. In addition, row house reconstruction has many peculiarities all its own. For example, theft from small, unprotected urban construction sites is a serious problem. How does a contractor determine a reasonable allowance for such an item? The estimates for such contingencies can be substantial, yet there is no standard which may be applied. The usual practice is to include a substantial percentage for overhead, profit, and "miscellaneous." This figure can run from 15% of the job's direct cost to 50% or more.

4. Labor

One immediate advantage of small-scale rehabilitation (usually where construction contracts are less than $200,000) is the contractor's ability to employ nonunion labor. The resulting cost savings can be as much as 20% below the levels of union work; however, productivity of nonunion labor is often lower, which lengthens the construction period.

Union labor is rarely employed in row house renovation due to the cost of such labor being more than its nonunion counterpart, and most unions overlook these projects because the amount of "lost business" is small.

5. Performance Bonds

A performance bond for new construction usually costs the contractor about 1% on the first $100,000 of contract value. Since the contractor's net worth and reputation influence this item significantly, a relatively small or unknown contractor might have to pay between 2 and 3% of the first $100,000 for the same bond. Some small contractors are not bondable themselves for the lack of experience demanded by a bonding company. These firms, then, must ally themselves with suppliers whose credit will be used to "back-up" the bond; the bond can then cost the owner up to 5% of the job cost. Obviously the prudent owner should discuss alternatives with his architect.

6. Special Cost Items

Wherever possible the owner involved in a rehabilitation should be alert to additional expenditures that may be incurred during construction. Even with the greatest caution these so-called "extras" frequently are unavoidable, thereby becoming necessities rather than extras. In other instances, however, extra costs are the result of personal preferences and should be carefully weighed and justified before being approved. Two different examples may be cited: the first, an integral structural problem — the second, an optional feature.

Floor joist replacement can be especially costly. When joists are found to have insecure headers or longitudinal splits or notches resulting from poor plumbing installations they must be replaced. At a price level of about $100 per 3" x 10" or 3" x 12" joist (including the removal of the defective timber), this type of extra is expensive.

Similarly, converting fireplaces to woodburning condition can involve substantial sums of money. To rebuild fireplaces, the fireplace frame and mantel must be removed, and the flue must be exposed and lined (the latter usually required by local codes, or dictated by good construction practice), the firebox must be rebuilt, a new hearth laid, and both the frame and mantel either rebuilt or replaced. According to rule-of-thumb estimates, the cost generally ends up as $150 or more per flue, per floor. Applying this formula to a three-story building with a garden floor apartment, and two fireplaces per floor, the resulting charge is $300 for the garden floor, $600 for the first floor, etc., with an approximate total of $3,000 for the entire fireplace rebuilding project, and after all this work the fireplaces may not draw well!

7. Structural Unknowns

In spite of the most careful scrutiny of the building prior to its purchase, many undisclosed defects become apparent as internal demolition proceeds. These may be classified as: defective timbers, old equipment requiring removal, deteriorated or porous foundation walls, dry-rot and mold, etc. Also, new utility hook-ups may be required, necessitating digging up the sidewalk and street, an extremely expensive and time-consuming operation. Obviously all of these items will add to the total cost, either as inclusions in the bid or as extras.

8. Roof Bond

A 15- or 20-year bonded roof may be difficult or impossible to obtain, or ultimately may cost as much as the entire roofing job itself, due to the generally small square foot area involved. It is the responsibility of the architect to consider alternatives such as a guarantee to a high-priced bond.

9. Utilities

Does the code, or good practice, require a back-water valve on the house sewer? To install one after the sewer is in can cost $200 or more. Is the original sewer usable, or must it be replaced? The cost of a 50- to 80-foot horizontal run of cast iron pipe generally comes high. Are there shut-off valves on the domestic water line (and sprinkler line, if the building has one) in the street, or in the building? Frequently, row houses were constructed without such valves. (No problem, but wait until the first leak!) Is the electric trench or duct (and sleeve) sufficient to carry the increased wire size underground to the service panel? This item is frequently overlooked, especially for all-electric buildings with heavy service lines.

10. Compliance with the Building Code and its Interpretation by the Inspector

Plan examiners in the building department are human and, therefore, may err. In a recent case the building inspector refused to approve the issuance of a Certificate of Occupancy until a protected skylight was installed in the roof over the public stairs. Although the plan examiner had overlooked this item, it cost the owner an extra $300.

11. Air Conditioners

The installation of sleeved, through-the-wall air conditioners may be complicated by unremovable sections of masonry on the building's facade or

The grand facade of this luxurious limestone row house is defeated by the window air-conditioners. Occasionally the masonry under the window can be cut to accept the air-conditioner, but this is an expensive alternative.

window sills too low to accommodate the equipment. The alternatives are either unattractive window-mounted air conditioners, or a central system costing $4000 or more.

12. Floor Joists

Spacing of existing joists can cause front-to-back displacement of the plumbing "stack" and ductwork for bath and kitchen fans up to 12 inches either way. What will this do to room size and other refinements incorporated into the plans? An insistence upon the plan as drawn to the inch can be troublesome for the contractor and expensive for the owner.

The list seems endless for each row house has its own peculiarities, its own liabilities, and various plans proposed by different owners further complicate the situation. Nevertheless, each phase of renovation and each factor involved must be scrutinized and carefully estimated as to practicality and cost.

ROW HOUSE RENOVATION COST GUIDELINES

The listing of approximate renovation costs appearing below should be used with great care to avoid misinterpretation. This listing offers only general figures, and the reader is strongly advised to solicit bids from local contractors rather than to rely too heavily on any figure he may compute from this table, or any others that may appear in print in other media.

AVERAGE RENOVATION COSTS PER SQUARE FOOT FOR NEW YORK

	Low Quality	Medium Quality	High Quality
Demolition	$ .55	$ .60	$ .60
Masonry	1.60	1.80	2.00
Carpentry	1.75	2.00	2.50
Windows	.50	.60	.80
Doors/frames	.40	.45	.50
Stairs (not entire replacement)	.10	.15	.20
Plaster/drywall	1.90	2.00	2.50
Electric	.75	.90	1.20
Heating	1.20	1.30	1.50
Air conditioning	.40	.45	.70
Plumbing	1.40	1.50	1.75
Kitchens	.60	.75	1.25
Insulation, roofing, sheet-metal	.40	.45	.50
Miscellaneous iron	.10	.15	.25
Floors – average all areas	.70	.75	1.00
Tile	.25	.30	.40
Painting	.50	.75	1.25
Hardware	.10	.15	.30
Square foot total costs (renovation only)	$13.20	$15.05	$19.20

The preceding costs are presented with certain assumptions:

1. All ceiling heights in the building average about 10 feet.
2. A cost figure from the table must be applied to all floor areas (including basement) of the subject building.
3. Individual unit prices per trade may be substantially different from those that will be experienced by the reader, due to extremes in plans or specifications, but they have been computed to represent an average level.
4. These costs are for renovation only: they assume repair of or retention of the building's shell; and include complete demolition and reconstruction of the building interior.

SPECIFIC ROW HOUSE RENOVATION COSTS

To convey to the reader some idea of the amount and distribution of row house renovation costs on a specific project, the following itemized list is presented as it pertained to a recent four-story building renovated to include two floor-through apartments and an owner's duplex.

1.	Demolition and Excavation	$ 9,000
2.	Masonry and concrete	10,000
3.	Steel	2,500
4.	Roofing and flashing	1,200
5.	Rough carpentry	13,500
6.	Lath, plaster and drywall	17,000
7.	Finish carpentry, doors and windows	18,000
8.	Cabinet work	2,000
9.	Wood flooring	3,500
10.	Hardware	1,000
11.	Ceramic tile and stone work	2,400
12.	Painting of interior and exterior	5,000
13.	Equipment (refrigerator, washer-dryer, ranges, dishwashers, medicine cabinets, etc.)	4,400
14.	Heating and air conditioning	6,000
15.	Ventilation (ducts, fans, dampers)	1,800
16.	Plumbing	11,000
17.	Electrical	8,500
18.	Clean-up and miscellaneous, such as permits, certificate of occupancy, etc.	1,300
	Total cost	$118,000

Chapter 16
Security

Nothing can more effectively ruin an otherwise pleasant weekend away from home than a burglary committed in one's absence, and the incident introduces a certain note of terror into the victim's life that is apt to persist for many months afterward. Although a thief, with enough time and ingenuity, can enter almost any apartment, it is obviously the owner's obligation to try and protect himself as best he can. Even simple security planning prior to construction pays dividends in peace of mind, and a thief discovering some protective measures may pass on to another less well-protected building and try there instead.

Row house security planning may be divided into "outside" and "inside" sections, and both depend upon careful preconstruction planning and organization.

OUTSIDE SECURITY

Bars and Gates

Window bars and gates are classified in three categories, and the degree of security varies directly with the type of construction and price.

1. Lightweight Gates. The least expensive, and also the least secure, are light gauge, pressed metal, accordion-type gates. When extended across the window, they produce bars spaced 4 inches to 6 inches apart in a diamond pattern and are secured with one or two small padlocks. While there is some degree of protection against intrusion, these gates are more suited to keeping children in when the window is open than to keeping burglars out. An average installation costs $50 to $100 per opening, plus locks.

2. Heavy-duty Moveable Gates. A much more secure type of gate, although somewhat similar in design to the first, is constructed of much heavier and stronger metal with spacings of only 2 inches to 3 inches between the diagonal bars. This type usually rolls back and forth on a steel bar at the

Ornamental ironwork often was added to a building both as a functional element, a railing, and as a decorative element, a window guard. The security provided by the latter is far from complete.

bottom and within a similar track at the top of the opening. These gates are suited to windows and terrace or garden doors and resemble the storefront protective devices found in the commercial sections of many cities. They are locked with at least two padlocks, which should be "hardened shackle" variety costing $10 - $15 each depending upon size. Since it may be illegal to place a locked gate in front of any door or window leading to a fire escape, a special gate may be procured for this purpose, which does not require a lock and key, and is easily released from the inside in case of an emergency.

When opened, these sliding accordion gates are much less prisonlike in appearance than fixed bars, and they may be folded back against the sides of door or window when not locked. Usually the bottom track also folds up locking the gate firmly against accidental release. In spite of the extra cost, insist that each gate be installed with an extra-heavy-duty, U-shaped channel at the bottom; without it the gate is much less secure, and it is much easier for an intruder to force apart the vertical bars and squeeze through. These gates cost about $30 per foot of width, with a premium paid for special heights, or special frames.

Some consideration should be given to gate mountings and color. Inside mounting provides less chance of rust and corrosion, while outside mounting is less noticeable from the inside. The owner must decide which he prefers. Standard colors are usually black and aluminum, but other neutral colors are also obtainable. While these neutral colors may be more preferable, they add to the cost. These gates, especially those installed on the outside, should be opened and closed several times a year and the pivots and padlocks well lubricated. This prevents rust collecting in the joints and does not permit the gate to freeze in position.

3. *Permanent Gate Installations.* The most secure gate is one that is permanently affixed to the building on the outside of the window. These are usually constructed of 3/8-inch or 1/2-inch round, or square, steel bars set vertically about 4 inches apart. The bars are welded in holes punched or drilled into the stone sill. This additional feature is not usually included in new installations because the extra drilling and proper alignment of the bars is expensive.

Permanent gates can be mounted in two ways. In the first method, the ends of the horizontal members are screwed to the window frame on the outside; the screw heads are then covered with wood trim on the sides. This is the simplest but least secure method. Alternatively, holes are drilled laterally into the sides of the masonry window opening, outside the window frame, but inside the outer edge of the masonry opening. Short steel pins are then inserted in the holes, and the gate is either bolted or welded to the pins. Welding provides almost absolute security. Costs vary from $150 to $200 per average window, depending upon construction and the method used in mounting. Hinged gates for garden or terrace doors ($200 up, depending upon size) can be fabricated to match the window bars. These bars and gates can also be painted, and with fewer heavier pieces maintenance is a relatively minor problem compared to accordion gates.

Instead of being restricted to the conventional type of gate currently on the market, there may be a possibility of installing original ironwork, more in keeping with the building's architecture and style. Gates with distinctive wrought-iron design dating from the late 1800's may be obtained from other neighborhood buildings undergoing reconstruction. However, this is only possible where "complete" renovations occur and where the owner has decided to remove and discard such ornamental elements. This ironwork will probably be covered with a thick coat of old paint. It may be repainted; this is the least expensive, but least satisfactory method. A far better method would be to remove the old paint before refinishing. This may be accomplished in several ways: scraping by hand, using a blowtorch and putty knife, or applying paint remover. All three procedures are arduous, tedious, and time-consuming, but relatively inexpensive. A much more satisfactory and durable method, though more expensive, is to sandblast the ironwork and then prime paint it with red lead.

Regardless of what method is adopted, when cut to fit the openings, repainted, and finally secured, original ironwork can add greatly to the beauty of the building.

Entrance Door and Foyer

Buildings built between 1850 and 1920 often had two sets of outside doors; one glazed set, opening outward, afforded the same sort of protection as that obtained from today's storm doors. If they still remain, it is advisable to discard them as a hazard. A high wind is apt to catch them sometimes with enough force to shatter the glass. Furthermore, they are difficult to weatherstrip properly, and they ultimately turn out to be just one more item requiring maintenance. The set of inner doors are by far more important. They are constructed either entirely of wood panels, or are half-paneled and half-glazed. Row houses built prior to 1850 generally had only one set of doors, opening inward; as a rule, they were partially solid, and partially glazed. If in restorable condition, these outer doors are worth the trouble and expense to bring them back to their original condition, not only because of their function, but also because they conform with the architecture of the building's facade.

The door that separates the foyer from the lobby is usually found to be partially glazed often with fixed side lights and a transom. Since this door is invariably sturdier and more secure than any modern replacement, it should be restored whenever possible. This is the door with the "buzzer" (solenoid latch and strike plate) and warrants attention because of its high security value. The latch is mounted in the door jamb and can cost all the way from $10 to $100, uninstalled. The wise owner will choose the best to be found on the market for obvious reasons. Most row houses converted into apartments, and many of those renovated for owner occupancy and apartments, unwisely depend upon an inexpensive latch, one that can be forced by a medium-sized screwdriver. To their extreme regret, many owners soon discover that this is a great mistake. The lock and the knob, together with the latch, should cost the better part of $200 installed, if they are to be of any real value as security. In combination with a good ($50) door closer, these several items serve as important factors in row house safety. In addition, light steel guards may be installed on the inside of the transom, side lights, and the door window. However, forcing the door seems to be the favorite method of burglars, who evidently fear that the sound of breaking glass will betray their attempts at entry.

Closed Circuit Television

In conjunction with the above standard features, closed circuit television from the foyer to each apartment adds immeasureably to the security of a building but it is extremely expensive. The quality of the TV equipment can affect its price, but whether of high or low quality, it is always expensive. The camera will cost from $250 to $500, and the receivers in each apartment will range from $100 to $225. The higher quality equipment has a shorter warm-up time, will operate much longer without malfunction, and generally will give a clearer picture.

Instead of considering this costly equipment, for $40 enough coaxial cable can be purchased to provide a line from the foyer to the first apartment and then one-by-one to the top floor. With an electrical outlet located near each apartment door, as well as in the foyer, closed circuit TV can be added at some later time—budget permitting—with no accompanying unsightly wires. One of the main arguments in favor of this type of security is its identification potential. A significant number of theives gain easy entry to buildings by merely buzzing. The trusting housewife who responds to a buzz by asking, "Who's there?" too often is satisfied with the customary dodge of "Laundry" or "package" and buzzes the intruder inside. To be sure he takes care to avoid visiting that particular apartment, for he knows that someone is there, others that might be empty are fair game. Closed circuit TV can permanently eliminate this hazard by providing easy means of instantly identifying the individual requesting entrance.

Roofs

Roof security is of prime importance. Police often admit that in many row house burglaries, thieves obtain entry via the roof. The greatest aid to such entries is a roof access hatch, generally reached by a steel ladder on the inside. These hatches are usually constructed of wood and often have deteriorated over the years. Owners should take care that they have a steel plate bolted to the underside; the hold-down hooks should be renewed with heavy duty, quick-release catches (in case of fire) bolted to the sides of the opening.

Most row houses have one or more skylights constructed of light metal and patterned glass. These probably will be in poor repair and will have to be replaced—if only to avoid leaks. Clear plastic domes are suitable as replacements, in most instances, especially if the construction calls for skylight relocation. Under such circumstances roof openings can be sized properly for the new skylight and costly custom-built sizes avoided.

Often the building code will call for protection of skylights with heavy wire-mesh screens, both over and under the skylight. The inside screen should extend well beyond the opening and be firmly affixed to the ceiling. This prevents burglars, who have already entered from above, from reaching the fasteners. Both roof hatch and skylights can be wired for alarms as an added precaution.

INSIDE SECURITY

Door Locks

Inside security basically concerns apartment door locks. A door lock has two principal parts: the cylinder, which provides an entry channel for the key, and the locking mechanism. The simplest form of lock is the spring latch or live-bolt type. If the building was formerly, or still is a rooming house, this is the type of lock most often found on the inside doors. It affords little or no protection since the latch can be pulled back with a strip of celluloid or spring steel, a credit card, or even a paper clip! A second and sturdier type is called a dead-bolt, which is a bar of steel activated by the key turning the cylinder on the outside and by a small handle turned on the inside. Many locks combine live- and dead-bolts into one unit allowing the occupant to engage the dead-bolt when leaving the apartment. The normal throw (i.e. horizontal projection when locked) of a dead-bolt is between ½-inch and ¾-inch, but a 1-inch throw is much better, making it more difficult to pry apart the door and its jamb. A third lock, widely sold by the Segal Lock Company and other firms, is a modification of the dead-bolt type. This lock usually has two bolts which are L-shaped and move sideways and then downward into holes or slots in the strike plate (the metal piece screwed to the door jamb). Thus the door is held to the jamb, and these bolts must "give" before the door can be successfully pried open.

Police Locks

Even though the original doors and frames may be in good enough condition to be retained and also may be in the desired position after the architect has finished the plans, shrinkage may have produced a space between door and jamb, or the frame or door may be insecure. This is when a police lock solves the problem. In this type when the key is turned, an angled solid bar of steel is moved into position as a wedge between the lock and a spot on the floor about two feet back of the door on the inside. A special fitting is required to hold this bar. For weakened doors this lock produces the same effect as the old-fashioned method of propping a chair under the knob.

Chain Locks

Door chains, as they are frequently called, have been favorites in the security area for decades due primarily to their low cost. They have a certain value in row houses, particularly when the door panels have been reinforced by a piece of heavy-gauge aluminum, or light-gauge steel, bolted to the inside of the door. A chain lock consists of a length of chain, permanently fastened to the jamb, with a fitting on the loose end that rides in a track screwed to the inside of the door itself. The door must be closed to disengage this type of fastener. These chains should be made of welded links; those that are not can be easily forced open. Some chain locks are manufactured with key-operated locking devices which may be secured from the outside. If the door is opened by forcing the door lock, the chain lock will at least offer just one more obstacle to entry.

Lock Cylinders

Cylinders are the heart of a locking mechanism. The proper key inserted and turned in a cylinder will activate whichever lock is found on the door. The ordinary key "kicks" five or more "pins" into alignment, and permits the cylinder to turn. Such a cylinder can be picked by a professional in a matter of minutes. However, there are on the market about a half-dozen special cylinders, each requiring its own special key. One is magnetic, one employs three rows of pins, etc.; all of these special key-cylinder combinations are patented, and purchasers are registered to control unauthorized key orders.

Since special cylinders, keys and other unusual locking devices often complicate the contractor's access during construction, a practical approach is to have him install inexpensive normal cylinders, which may be changed later to suit the owner. However, cylinder guards may be installed during the construction period. These are 1/8-inch steel plates that are bolted with carriage bolts (round smooth head) to the front of the door and cover the cylinder, except for a small hole designed for the key.

It is difficult to properly lock sliding doors, and in order to properly lock a particular door, the owner should discuss the situation with a lock manufacturer, the door supplier, or with the contractor before actual construction commences.

Living in a building with other tenants demands a sensible lock and key policy. Most owners insist on being able to enter other apartments in case of an emergency. Nevertheless, a total locking system will have to be devised whereby the tenant will be able to maintain his own personal security while at the same time permitting access to other apartments on the part of the owner when necessary.

MISCELLANEOUS SECURITY FEATURES

1. Viewers

Door viewers, a common item in security, are inexpensive, and while not particularly attractive, they provide an effective means of identifying the individual outside the apartment without opening the door itself.

2. Chains

Some row houses were built with a steel "engineer's hatch," located under the stoop. This allowed access to the cellar without entering any other part of the house, and was used primarily by maintenance and repair men, usually when the house was occupied by a single family. Since they exist, they must be secured. To do this a heavy chain should be passed through a hole in the hatch, or secured to the handle on the underside and then wrapped around an inside pipe or some sturdy stationary object. The ends of the chain should be padlocked.

3. Safes

It is extremely doubtful whether home safes are as dependable as most individuals think. In many ways safes can prove to be a nuisance, and the smaller varieties are frequently carried off by thieves. In this period of widespread branch banking, it would seem that bank facilities are much safer than any home safe. However, if after due consideration there is justification for installing a home safe, the owner should realize that if he is not prepared to spend upward of $200, his safe will prove more fireproof than burglarproof. Common practice is to choose some suitable location for the safe where it may be permanently anchored to the building frame. This should be done prior to the installation of plasterboard or plaster.

4. Alarms

House alarms serve two major purposes: to alert those responsible in case of fire and to inform neighbors or outside protective agencies that an attempt at illegal entry is being made. There is the possibility too that the noise of the alarm may ward off the intruder.

Alarms come in a large variety of types, shapes, capacities, and prices, but there are two basic systems to consider and either one may entitle the owner to an insurance discount. The most expensive of the two is the alarm device which, when a circuit is broken or a sensor activated, alerts a monitor at another location. The traditional system of this type has been marketed for years by firms such as the Holmes Electric Protective Company. However, most yellow pages will list other companies servicing similar or related devices.

Some firms "wire" the doors and windows of a building as well as provide one or more "panic" buttons—extremely valuable in emergencies. Average costs for such systems installed in a renovated row house are from $1200 to $3000. For monitored protection monthly charges range from $10 to $40 per apartment, per building. As a note of caution, unless the agency is immediately notified of a "false alarm," an armed guard or the police will arrive within a matter of minutes!

A somewhat less expensive central system depends upon a broken circuit that triggers a telephone dialing device. This arrangement provides up to five dialings of telephone numbers each accompanied by a recorded message such as, "A burglary is in progress at ..." Most effective results are obtained when this system is programmed to dial in succession three nearby friends, rather then the local police precinct, where administrative delays may be encountered. In addition to the low four-figure investment in required wiring, the automatic telephone dialing device alone can cost from $200 to $500.

A "Local" alarm system depends upon one that rings bells, sounds horns, or flashes lights on or near the building. While the average city dweller is somewhat immune to such disturbances, one that operates intermittently is certain to draw his attention. If every apartment entrance door is wired into this system, a delay mechanism will have to be built in to avoid awakening the neighbors every time a tenant returns home. In addition the timer should turn off the alarm after a certain interval and automatically reset it for future use.

Choosing a particular alarm system can be postponed until late in construction, or during early occupancy. However, if the wiring is carefully planned beforehand, subsequent installation will be easier and much less unsightly. Few row houses are wired for alarms, but the increasing sophistication of today's criminals calls for more attention to this important phase of security even though its total cost may ultimately range into the thousands of dollars.

This elegant row house dining room was created by preserving existing architectural details in relatively good condition, rather than massive renovation. (Photo © 1979 by Jim Kalett)

Chapter 17
Telephone Installation and Service

Most telephone companies are reasonably cooperative with owners of row houses undergoing renovation who wish to conceal interior telephone wires inside partitions. The telephone companies distinguish between two distinct services: one which is provided during construction and one upon occupancy.

WIRING DURING CONSTRUCTION

Prewiring

The telephone company will install, upon request and without charge, vertical wires in a building. This wiring provides service to the front and rear portions of each floor and includes the installation of a junction box in the basement with a hook-up, often to the backyard cable. On each floor the wires run to a terminal located inside an appropriate closet. The number of tenants or type of service is not a concern at the time of installation, and either the owner or the contractor can arrange for this work.

Concealed Advance Wiring

Later in construction but before both sides of the interior partitions are covered, the owner may wish to have horizontal telephone wires run to approximate location of each wall outlet. The telephone company must have an application for service from the eventual occupant before this wiring can be done. This arcane regulation prevents concealed advance wiring, except upon the identification and designation of an occupant or owner prior to completion of construction.

INSTALLATION OF EQUIPMENT

The installation of telephone equipment occurs after completion of construction prior to or simultaneous with occupancy. In addition to being familiar with the normal types of installations, the row house owner should be aware of four additional service possibilities that present opportunities especially during construction:

1. The telephone company can prewire or advance wire for more than one circuit thus allowing two or more separate lines in each apartment. This eliminates the necessity of installing a second line on the surface at a late date, and alarm systems with telephone dialers can be accommodated.
2. Touch-tone telephones may require special extra-conductor wire larger in diameter than regular wire and consequently more unsightly when installed on the surface at a later time.
3. Wire can be easily run to obscure locations for later installation of wall telephones, without causing unnecessary installation problems. For example, with advance planning a wall telephone can be mounted on a ceramic tile wall with the wire concealed.
4. If there is a deck, garden, or terrace, weathertight outside jack connections can be planned.

The local telephone company service representative will be able to supply fuller details as well as provide information about the various types of service, color of equipment, monthly costs, installation charges, etc.

Chapter 18
General Operation After Renovation

Operating expenses (or carrying charges, as they often are called) vary according to the particular row house, and depend upon the rent roll and the space occupied by the owner. This estimated figure should have been prepared before any offers to purchase were made, otherwise there is the danger of not having a sufficient flow of cash to cover post-construction costs. Since every family head—and the row house is no exception—must decide how much money may be put aside for his monthly rental, there are definite limits to be respected. Some individuals intending to occupy space in the completed building seem to take it for granted that once his other apartments are all rented, the total income will be adequate to cover the imputed rent for his own space. Unfortunately, this is not always true, especially when the owner's family occupies more than one floor. A sample statement of operations is seen in the following hypothetical example of a newly renovated, four-story building, where the owner lives in the lower duplex (with garden), and the four upper apartments (two, one-room units and two effeciency units) produce a total annual income of $14,000.

Estimated carrying charges are as follows:

First mortgage $80,000; constant monthly payment of 8½% interest, 2½% amortization	$8,800
Second mortgage $30,000; constant monthly payment of 8½% interest, 2½% amortization (probably with a due date in 3 to 10 years)	3,300
Taxes	3,000
Fuel: #2 Oil	1,500
Gas and electric, halls and owner's apartment	500
Water and sewer charges	200
Repairs and maintenance allowance	800
Superintendent	600
Insurance	600
Total expenses	$19,300
Rent roll	14,000
Annual loss	$ 5,300

Thus the owner's approximate monthly carrying charge is $441 while amortizing the mortgages.

RENT

Apartment rents should be figured carefully. First, the rent must be one a tenant is able to pay; secondly, the figure should be commensurate with rentals being asked for similar quarters, thereby insuring constant and continued occupancy; thirdly, the owner is justified in expecting a fair return on his total investment, including a pro-rated portion of the maintenance costs.

RENT COLLECTION

Some owners prefer to make their own rent collections, believing that this is a way of maintaining friendly neighborly relations. At the same time owners feel that they may become alerted to incipient problems which, if promptly attended to, might be prevented from becoming emergencies later on.

Other owners prefer a more formal arrangement whereby a real estate agent or management firm is employed to collect the rents. Such an agent will agree to manage the property and will charge from 5 to 10% of the gross rent roll. However, for smaller buildings, if the agent considers this charge insufficient in return for what is demanded of him, he may ask a monthly minimum fee for his time and effort.

RENT INCREASES

Most owners institute rent increases under justifiable circumstances. Some increases result from situations beyond an owner's control, such as higher property taxes, increased maintenance charges, or some unexpected expense for emergencies (i.e. broken water main, extensive roof repairs, boiler replacement, etc.). Occasionally some portion of the total expenditure is pro-rated among the tenants in the form of rent increases as leases expire.

For unrenovated buildings, prior to reconstruction, there are other types of justifiable rent increases which are not the result of unexpected emergencies, but rather result from a particular action taken by the owner. He may be entitled, under city, state, or federal laws, to increase rent for a variety of real estate improvements, either in individual apartments, or throughout an entire building. For example, the installation of new kitchen facilities (stove, sink, refrigerator, etc.) constitutes a major improvement, and may qualify for a rent increase. Entire building improvements, such as rewiring, new plumbing, a new heating plant, etc., also are included in this category of major capital improvement.

Before undertaking any such improvements the owner is expected to submit his plans and justification in detail to the proper governing body. The question of tenant's consent to the increase should be cleared at the same time; it may, or may not be required.

Chapter 19
Owner-Tenant Relations

Most owners should realize that renovating a row house is similar to any other form of real estate venture, and a return on investment in the form of rental income is necessary not only to repay the money borrowed for the project, but also to provide some profit on the capital invested. As a direct result, many row houses are reconstructed with living quarters for the owner and apartments for tenants, or all apartments rented to tenants with the owner living elsewhere.

Nominally, row house apartment rentals may be slightly in excess of new building rentals, in addition to which there are sometimes certain restrictions imposed by the owner. Particularly in smaller projects, the individual responsible for having undertaken the reconstruction of the building will be discriminating in certain ways (although in most cities he may not discriminate against race or creed if he has three or more units). If he insists on couples without children, that is his prerogative. If he refuses to rent to single, unmarried persons, that too, is his right. In like manner, the type of individual apt to be attracted by row house living is definitely not an average person. He is probably searching for something individualistic, something quite different from an ordinary apartment, new or old. Because of these demands and the uniqueness of a building the renter is usually willing to pay something more than what ordinarily might be expected as rent for an equivalent apartment in a new building.

Under such circumstances, both parties must exercise good judgment before agreeing to any rental, since occupying a renovated row house apartment can be comparable to cooperative living. Contacts are apt to be much closer and friendlier than those characterizing average city apartments. It is practically impossible for any tenant to avoid the owner, and vice versa. The prospective tenant will have to rely upon his insight into human nature to guide him; the owner has other, more factual data to influence his decision.

SELECTING A TENANT

The owner is within his rights to ask for personal as well as employment references. Much like any other lessor, the owner also may ask for the

Many row houses have some form of exterior architectural embellishment like these brownstone carvings. (Photo © 1979 by Jim Kalett)

names of banks which know the individual. Thoroughly investigating this information, as well as checking the applicant's credit rating, the owner then is in a position to ascertain whether the applicant may be considered a sound prospect.

Since row house living is to a certain degree communal in character, the owner may want to learn where the individual presently lives, where he previously lived, how long he lived in these various locations, what rent was paid, the size of the apartments, and why he is interested in making the current change. The prospective lessee can in no way take exception to these questions since the same list may be requested by any reputable real estate agent. If there should be any possibility of actually visiting the prospect before any definite commitment has been made it is highly recommended. Spending even five minutes in a home is sufficient to convey a clear impression of the occupant's living habits. Such impressions are often more informative about personality than a folder of references.

If he intends to occupy space in the building the owner must be assured in his own mind that the individual seeking occupancy will be able to accommodate himself to the general tenor of the building. Perhaps one of the more natural ways for the owner to achieve this basic understanding is to show his own apartment to the prospective tenant; at the same time he might make casual reference to the other occupants, their occupations, their interests, etc. This will subtly convey the general building atmosphere to the individual, with emphasis upon mutual consideration and the maintenance of orderliness and cleanliness, and the applicant's conversation may help the owner to make a decision.

There are a number of items which should be covered with the applicant such as the question of pets, prompt payment of monthly rent, long-term guests, subleasing privileges, etc. — all of which must be discussed by both parties before a lease is proposed.

THE LEASE

It is recommended that one of the following be used:

1. A lease form prepared by the local real estate board if such a form exists. Usually an owner must be a member of the board to have access to such a lease.
2. A lease form may be purchased from a stationery store with a business supplies section.
3. An attorney can prepare a suitable lease.

In addition to the basic sections of these leases, the owner should include several clauses such as: (a) Only those tenants who sign the lease may reside in the premises. While this statement may occur in the printed section of the lease, repeating it lends added emphasis. (b) If the prospective tenant requests a sublease clause, and it is granted, the tenant should remain responsible for the subtenant's rent and the maintenance of the premises. Owners may also wish to have the right to approve sublessees. (c) One month's security must be paid, in addition to the normal month's rent, at the time of signing the lease. The security is returnable when the tenant vacates the premises, providing they are left in good condition and rent has been paid through the date of leaving. (d) The tenant is requested to submit a signed statement one month in advance of lease expiration, informing the owner that he does not expect to renew the lease.

OWNER-TENANT HARMONY

The owner is primarily interested in renting his vacant apartment to an individual who will pay the rent promptly. If the owner has used discretion and a degree of insight, he will have selected the proper person but disturbing incidents may occur, and these must be handled with discretion and firmness.

Although the tenant has been informed, for example, that loud radios and television sets should be turned down, and there should be no unnecessary noise after certain hours, there may be lapses. It is the owner's right to bring this to the attention of the tenant. Such action pertains to any disregard on the tenant's part of any lease clause. With tact, however, most situations should be resolved satisfactorily. On the other hand, if there are complaints from a tenant about the management of the building, it is the owner's obligation to attend to the matter immediately.

Prompt payment of rent is obligatory; if the tenant should delay rent payments unreasonably or habitually, eviction proceedings should commence by serving the delinquent tenant with a dispossess notice or following local procedure. If the tenant still refuses to pay rent, the owner has legal redress to complete the eviction proceedings. Usually the tenant will pay the back rent under these circumstances; however, should there be need to serve several and repeated dispossess notices over a period of months, some judges will order the tenant to vacate the premises because he has been a nuisance to the owner.

Chapter 20
Personal Property Insurance After Construction

Personal property insurance (often called contents insurance) is the responsibility of the individual tenant or of the owner for his own property. The widest coverage is obtained in a Homeowner's Tenants Policy which provides insurance on personal property for fire, extended coverages, theft, and personal liability insurance. In addition, this policy usually covers living expenses when the tenant is forced to temporarily relocate because of a loss through fire. A discount often applies to the above policy over coverage of the risks separately.

A tenant's policy can have additional coverages for jewelry, furs, fine arts, credit card loss, theft away from premises, etc. However, it is becoming increasingly difficult for residents of large cities to obtain personal property insurance because of the changing city scene. Insurance companies are reluctant to write such policies because of the high loss level they have experienced. With both members of a family away from the home for the major part of the day, illegal house entry has increased, and insurance companies are often not interested in this high risk. In some instances a claim-free past record or a nonworking spouse may qualify as an apartment dweller for this coverage.

Personal property insurance premiums vary from location to location and are written on a flat rate per thousand dollars of value covered. The basic policy described above with a $19,000 face value for an Eastern location would cost about $250 for three years with an additional premium of about $75 for three years for coverage of theft away from the premises. If the premiums are paid annually, they are usually slightly more than one-third of the three year premium. The rate per thousand dollars of coverage decreases up to $15,000, after which it remains constant per thousand dollars of coverage. For coverage under $10,000, the rate per thousand usually increases to the minimum allowable coverage of $8000. Premiums in smaller cities may probably be lower than those quoted above.

Appendices

Appendix 1

CHECK LIST OF FORMS OR DOCUMENTS WHICH MAY BE REQUIRED IN ROW HOUSE RENOVATION

1. Attorney's Retainer Agreement
2. Owner-Architect Agreement
3. Purchase Agreement
4. Violation Report
5. Survey
6. Title Insurance Company Report
7. Purchase Money Mortgage, if any; Subordination Agreement, if any
8. Insurance (binder)
9. Narrative Closing Letter
10. Closing Statement
11. Report of Change in Landlord Identity to Rent Commission
12. Building Department Change of Ownership and Managing Agent Form
13. Sales Tax Return
14. Oil Tank Permit Change – Fire Department
15. Plans
16. Specifications
17. Bids from Contractors
18. Mortgage Application and Commitment from Lending Institutions for Construction Mortgage and/or Permanent Mortgage. All Mortgage Closing Documents including Satisfaction or Subordination of Existing Mortgages, if required.
19. Fire Department Guidelines
20. Owner-Contractor Agreement
21. List of Required Information from Contractor
22. Building Permit Application – Architectural

23. Building Permit Application – Plumbing
24. Building Permit
25. Sewer Approval Required Items
26. Architect's Letter regarding Sewer
27. Plumber's Letter regarding Sewer
28. Owner's Letter regarding Mechanical Ventilation
29. Sprinkler Test Report
30. Steel Work Inspection Certificate
31. Certificate of Electrical Inspection
32. Certificate of the New York Board of Fire Underwriters
33. Certificate of Occupancy Application
34. Certificate of Occupancy
35. Contractor's Guarantee

Appendix 2

APPENDIX 2 127

THE AMERICAN INSTITUTE OF ARCHITECTS

AIA Document B141

Standard Form of Agreement Between Owner and Architect

1977 EDITION

THIS DOCUMENT HAS IMPORTANT LEGAL CONSEQUENCES; CONSULTATION WITH
AN ATTORNEY IS ENCOURAGED WITH RESPECT TO ITS COMPLETION OR MODIFICATION

AGREEMENT

made as of the   day of   in the year of Nineteen
Hundred and

BETWEEN the Owner:

and the Architect:

For the following Project:
(Include detailed description of Project location and scope.)

The Owner and the Architect agree as set forth below.

Copyright 1917, 1926, 1948, 1951, 1953, 1958, 1961, 1963, 1966, 1967, 1970, 1974, © 1977 by The American Institute of Architects, 1735 New York Avenue, N.W., Washington, D.C. 20006. Reproduction of the material herein or substantial quotation of its provisions without permission of the AIA violates the copyright laws of the United States and will be subject to legal prosecution.

AIA DOCUMENT B141 • OWNER-ARCHITECT AGREEMENT • THIRTEENTH EDITION • JULY 1977 • AIA® • © 1977
THE AMERICAN INSTITUTE OF ARCHITECTS, 1735 NEW YORK AVENUE, N.W., WASHINGTON, D.C. 20006   B141-1977   1

TERMS AND CONDITIONS OF AGREEMENT BETWEEN OWNER AND ARCHITECT

ARTICLE 1
ARCHITECT'S SERVICES AND RESPONSIBILITIES

BASIC SERVICES

The Architect's Basic Services consist of the five phases described in Paragraphs 1.1 through 1.5 and include normal structural, mechanical and electrical engineering services and any other services included in Article 15 as part of Basic Services.

1.1 SCHEMATIC DESIGN PHASE

1.1.1 The Architect shall review the program furnished by the Owner to ascertain the requirements of the Project and shall review the understanding of such requirements with the Owner.

1.1.2 The Architect shall provide a preliminary evaluation of the program and the Project budget requirements, each in terms of the other, subject to the limitations set forth in Subparagraph 3.2.1.

1.1.3 The Architect shall review with the Owner alternative approaches to design and construction of the Project.

1.1.4 Based on the mutually agreed upon program and Project budget requirements, the Architect shall prepare, for approval by the Owner, Schematic Design Documents consisting of drawings and other documents illustrating the scale and relationship of Project components.

1.1.5 The Architect shall submit to the Owner a Statement of Probable Construction Cost based on current area, volume or other unit costs.

1.2 DESIGN DEVELOPMENT PHASE

1.2.1 Based on the approved Schematic Design Documents and any adjustments authorized by the Owner in the program or Project budget, the Architect shall prepare, for approval by the Owner, Design Development Documents consisting of drawings and other documents to fix and describe the size and character of the entire Project as to architectural, structural, mechanical and electrical systems, materials and such other elements as may be appropriate.

1.2.2 The Architect shall submit to the Owner a further Statement of Probable Construction Cost.

1.3 CONSTRUCTION DOCUMENTS PHASE

1.3.1 Based on the approved Design Development Documents and any further adjustments in the scope or quality of the Project or in the Project budget authorized by the Owner, the Architect shall prepare, for approval by the Owner, Construction Documents consisting of Drawings and Specifications setting forth in detail the requirements for the construction of the Project.

1.3.2 The Architect shall assist the Owner in the preparation of the necessary bidding information, bidding forms, the Conditions of the Contract, and the form of Agreement between the Owner and the Contractor.

1.3.3 The Architect shall advise the Owner of any adjustments to previous Statements of Probable Construction Cost indicated by changes in requirements or general market conditions.

1.3.4 The Architect shall assist the Owner in connection with the Owner's responsibility for filing documents required for the approval of governmental authorities having jurisdiction over the Project.

1.4 BIDDING OR NEGOTIATION PHASE

1.4.1 The Architect, following the Owner's approval of the Construction Documents and of the latest Statement of Probable Construction Cost, shall assist the Owner in obtaining bids or negotiated proposals, and assist in awarding and preparing contracts for construction.

1.5 CONSTRUCTION PHASE—ADMINISTRATION OF THE CONSTRUCTION CONTRACT

1.5.1 The Construction Phase will commence with the award of the Contract for Construction and, together with the Architect's obligation to provide Basic Services under this Agreement, will terminate when final payment to the Contractor is due, or in the absence of a final Certificate for Payment or of such due date, sixty days after the Date of Substantial Completion of the Work, whichever occurs first.

1.5.2 Unless otherwise provided in this Agreement and incorporated in the Contract Documents, the Architect shall provide administration of the Contract for Construction as set forth below and in the edition of AIA Document A201, General Conditions of the Contract for Construction, current as of the date of this Agreement.

1.5.3 The Architect shall be a representative of the Owner during the Construction Phase, and shall advise and consult with the Owner. Instructions to the Contractor shall be forwarded through the Architect. The Architect shall have authority to act on behalf of the Owner only to the extent provided in the Contract Documents unless otherwise modified by written instrument in accordance with Subparagraph 1.5.16.

1.5.4 The Architect shall visit the site at intervals appropriate to the stage of construction or as otherwise agreed by the Architect in writing to become generally familiar with the progress and quality of the Work and to determine in general if the Work is proceeding in accordance with the Contract Documents. However, the Architect shall not be required to make exhaustive or continuous on-site inspections to check the quality or quantity of the Work. On the basis of such on-site observations as an architect, the Architect shall keep the Owner informed of the progress and quality of the Work, and shall endeavor to guard the Owner against defects and deficiencies in the Work of the Contractor.

1.5.5 The Architect shall not have control or charge of and shall not be responsible for construction means, methods, techniques, sequences or procedures, or for safety precautions and programs in connection with the Work, for the acts or omissions of the Contractor, Subcontractors or any other persons performing any of the Work, or for the failure of any of them to carry out the Work in accordance with the Contract Documents.

1.5.6 The Architect shall at all times have access to the Work wherever it is in preparation or progress.

1.5.7 The Architect shall determine the amounts owing to the Contractor based on observations at the site and on evaluations of the Contractor's Applications for Payment, and shall issue Certificates for Payment in such amounts, as provided in the Contract Documents.

1.5.8 The issuance of a Certificate for Payment shall constitute a representation by the Architect to the Owner, based on the Architect's observations at the site as provided in Subparagraph 1.5.4 and on the data comprising the Contractor's Application for Payment, that the Work has progressed to the point indicated; that, to the best of the Architect's knowledge, information and belief, the quality of the Work is in accordance with the Contract Documents (subject to an evaluation of the Work for conformance with the Contract Documents upon Substantial Completion, to the results of any subsequent tests required by or performed under the Contract Documents, to minor deviations from the Contract Documents correctable prior to completion, and to any specific qualifications stated in the Certificate for Payment); and that the Contractor is entitled to payment in the amount certified. However, the issuance of a Certificate for Payment shall not be a representation that the Architect has made any examination to ascertain how and for what purpose the Contractor has used the moneys paid on account of the Contract Sum.

1.5.9 The Architect shall be the interpreter of the requirements of the Contract Documents and the judge of the performance thereunder by both the Owner and Contractor. The Architect shall render interpretations necessary for the proper execution or progress of the Work with reasonable promptness on written request of either the Owner or the Contractor, and shall render written decisions, within a reasonable time, on all claims, disputes and other matters in question between the Owner and the Contractor relating to the execution or progress of the Work or the interpretation of the Contract Documents.

1.5.10 Interpretations and decisions of the Architect shall be consistent with the intent of and reasonably inferable from the Contract Documents and shall be in written or graphic form. In the capacity of interpreter and judge, the Architect shall endeavor to secure faithful performance by both the Owner and the Contractor, shall not show partiality to either, and shall not be liable for the result of any interpretation or decision rendered in good faith in such capacity.

1.5.11 The Architect's decisions in matters relating to artistic effect shall be final if consistent with the intent of the Contract Documents. The Architect's decisions on any other claims, disputes or other matters, including those in question between the Owner and the Contractor, shall be subject to arbitration as provided in this Agreement and in the Contract Documents.

1.5.12 The Architect shall have authority to reject Work which does not conform to the Contract Documents. Whenever, in the Architect's reasonable opinion, it is necessary or advisable for the implementation of the intent of the Contract Documents, the Architect will have authority to require special inspection or testing of the Work in accordance with the provisions of the Contract Documents, whether or not such Work be then fabricated, installed or completed.

1.5.13 The Architect shall review and approve or take other appropriate action upon the Contractor's submittals such as Shop Drawings, Product Data and Samples, but only for conformance with the design concept of the Work and with the information given in the Contract Documents. Such action shall be taken with reasonable promptness so as to cause no delay. The Architect's approval of a specific item shall not indicate approval of an assembly of which the item is a component.

1.5.14 The Architect shall prepare Change Orders for the Owner's approval and execution in accordance with the Contract Documents, and shall have authority to order minor changes in the Work not involving an adjustment in the Contract Sum or an extension of the Contract Time which are not inconsistent with the intent of the Contract Documents.

1.5.15 The Architect shall conduct inspections to determine the Dates of Substantial Completion and final completion, shall receive and forward to the Owner for the Owner's review written warranties and related documents required by the Contract Documents and assembled by the Contractor, and shall issue a final Certificate for Payment.

1.5.16 The extent of the duties, responsibilities and limitations of authority of the Architect as the Owner's representative during construction shall not be modified or extended without written consent of the Owner, the Contractor and the Architect.

1.6 PROJECT REPRESENTATION BEYOND BASIC SERVICES

1.6.1 If the Owner and Architect agree that more extensive representation at the site than is described in Paragraph 1.5 shall be provided, the Architect shall provide one or more Project Representatives to assist the Architect in carrying out such responsibilities at the site.

1.6.2 Such Project Representatives shall be selected, employed and directed by the Architect, and the Architect shall be compensated therefor as mutually agreed between the Owner and the Architect as set forth in an exhibit appended to this Agreement, which shall describe the duties, responsibilities and limitations of authority of such Project Representatives.

1.6.3 Through the observations by such Project Representatives, the Architect shall endeavor to provide further protection for the Owner against defects and deficiencies in the Work, but the furnishing of such project representation shall not modify the rights, responsibilities or obligations of the Architect as described in Paragraph 1.5.

1.7 ADDITIONAL SERVICES

The following Services are not included in Basic Services unless so identified in Article 15. They shall be provided if authorized or confirmed in writing by the Owner, and they shall be paid for by the Owner as provided in this Agreement, in addition to the compensation for Basic Services.

1.7.1 Providing analyses of the Owner's needs, and programming the requirements of the Project.

1.7.2 Providing financial feasibility or other special studies.

1.7.3 Providing planning surveys, site evaluations, environmental studies or comparative studies of prospective sites, and preparing special surveys, studies and submissions required for approvals of governmental authorities or others having jurisdiction over the Project.

1.7.4 Providing services relative to future facilities, systems and equipment which are not intended to be constructed during the Construction Phase.

1.7.5 Providing services to investigate existing conditions or facilities or to make measured drawings thereof, or to verify the accuracy of drawings or other information furnished by the Owner.

1.7.6 Preparing documents of alternate, separate or sequential bids or providing extra services in connection with bidding, negotiation or construction prior to the completion of the Construction Documents Phase, when requested by the Owner.

1.7.7 Providing coordination of Work performed by separate contractors or by the Owner's own forces.

1.7.8 Providing services in connection with the work of a construction manager or separate consultants retained by the Owner.

1.7.9 Providing Detailed Estimates of Construction Cost, analyses of owning and operating costs, or detailed quantity surveys or inventories of material, equipment and labor.

1.7.10 Providing interior design and other similar services required for or in connection with the selection, procurement or installation of furniture, furnishings and related equipment.

1.7.11 Providing services for planning tenant or rental spaces.

1.7.12 Making revisions in Drawings, Specifications or other documents when such revisions are inconsistent with written approvals or instructions previously given, are required by the enactment or revision of codes, laws or regulations subsequent to the preparation of such documents or are due to other causes not solely within the control of the Architect.

1.7.13 Preparing Drawings, Specifications and supporting data and providing other services in connection with Change Orders to the extent that the adjustment in the Basic Compensation resulting from the adjusted Construction Cost is not commensurate with the services required of the Architect, provided such Change Orders are required by causes not solely within the control of the Architect.

1.7.14 Making investigations, surveys, valuations, inventories or detailed appraisals of existing facilities, and services required in connection with construction performed by the Owner.

1.7.15 Providing consultation concerning replacement of any Work damaged by fire or other cause during construction, and furnishing services as may be required in connection with the replacement of such Work.

1.7.16 Providing services made necessary by the default of the Contractor, or by major defects or deficiencies in the Work of the Contractor, or by failure of performance of either the Owner or Contractor under the Contract for Construction.

1.7.17 Preparing a set of reproducible record drawings showing significant changes in the Work made during construction based on marked-up prints, drawings and other data furnished by the Contractor to the Architect.

1.7.18 Providing extensive assistance in the utilization of any equipment or system such as initial start-up or testing, adjusting and balancing, preparation of operation and maintenance manuals, training personnel for operation and maintenance, and consultation during operation.

1.7.19 Providing services after issuance to the Owner of the final Certificate for Payment, or in the absence of a final Certificate for Payment, more than sixty days after the Date of Substantial Completion of the Work.

1.7.20 Preparing to serve or serving as an expert witness in connection with any public hearing, arbitration proceeding or legal proceeding.

1.7.21 Providing services of consultants for other than the normal architectural, structural, mechanical and electrical engineering services for the Project.

1.7.22 Providing any other services not otherwise included in this Agreement or not customarily furnished in accordance with generally accepted architectural practice.

1.8 TIME

1.8.1 The Architect shall perform Basic and Additional Services as expeditiously as is consistent with professional skill and care and the orderly progress of the Work. Upon request of the Owner, the Architect shall submit for the Owner's approval a schedule for the performance of the Architect's services which shall be adjusted as required as the Project proceeds, and shall include allowances for periods of time required for the Owner's review and approval of submissions and for approvals of authorities having jurisdiction over the Project. This schedule, when approved by the Owner, shall not, except for reasonable cause, be exceeded by the Architect.

ARTICLE 2

THE OWNER'S RESPONSIBILITIES

2.1 The Owner shall provide full information regarding requirements for the Project including a program, which shall set forth the Owner's design objectives, constraints and criteria, including space requirements and relationships, flexibility and expandability, special equipment and systems and site requirements.

2.2 If the Owner provides a budget for the Project it shall include contingencies for bidding, changes in the Work during construction, and other costs which are the responsibility of the Owner, including those described in this Article 2 and in Subparagraph 3.1.2. The Owner shall, at the request of the Architect, provide a statement of funds available for the Project, and their source.

2.3 The Owner shall designate, when necessary, a representative authorized to act in the Owner's behalf with respect to the Project. The Owner or such authorized representative shall examine the documents submitted by the Architect and shall render decisions pertaining thereto promptly, to avoid unreasonable delay in the progress of the Architect's services.

2.4 The Owner shall furnish a legal description and a certified land survey of the site, giving, as applicable, grades and lines of streets, alleys, pavements and adjoining property; rights-of-way, restrictions, easements, encroachments, zoning, deed restrictions, boundaries and contours of the site; locations, dimensions and complete data pertaining to existing buildings, other improvements and trees; and full information concerning available service and utility lines both public and private, above and below grade, including inverts and depths.

2.5 The Owner shall furnish the services of soil engineers or other consultants when such services are deemed necessary by the Architect. Such services shall include test borings, test pits, soil bearing values, percolation tests, air and water pollution tests, ground corrosion and resistivity tests, including necessary operations for determining subsoil, air and water conditions, with reports and appropriate professional recommendations.

2.6 The Owner shall furnish structural, mechanical, chemical and other laboratory tests, inspections and reports as required by law or the Contract Documents.

2.7 The Owner shall furnish all legal, accounting and insurance counseling services as may be necessary at any time for the Project, including such auditing services as the Owner may require to verify the Contractor's Applications for Payment or to ascertain how or for what purposes the Contractor uses the moneys paid by or on behalf of the Owner.

2.8 The services, information, surveys and reports required by Paragraphs 2.4 through 2.7 inclusive shall be furnished at the Owner's expense, and the Architect shall be entitled to rely upon the accuracy and completeness thereof.

2.9 If the Owner observes or otherwise becomes aware of any fault or defect in the Project or nonconformance with the Contract Documents, prompt written notice thereof shall be given by the Owner to the Architect.

2.10 The Owner shall furnish required information and services and shall render approvals and decisions as expeditiously as necessary for the orderly progress of the Architect's services and of the Work.

ARTICLE 3

CONSTRUCTION COST

3.1 DEFINITION

3.1.1 The Construction Cost shall be the total cost or estimated cost to the Owner of all elements of the Project designed or specified by the Architect.

3.1.2 The Construction Cost shall include at current market rates, including a reasonable allowance for overhead and profit, the cost of labor and materials furnished by the Owner and any equipment which has been designed, specified, selected or specially provided for by the Architect.

3.1.3 Construction Cost does not include the compensation of the Architect and the Architect's consultants, the cost of the land, rights-of-way, or other costs which are the responsibility of the Owner as provided in Article 2.

3.2 RESPONSIBILITY FOR CONSTRUCTION COST

3.2.1 Evaluations of the Owner's Project budget, Statements of Probable Construction Cost and Detailed Estimates of Construction Cost, if any, prepared by the Architect, represent the Architect's best judgment as a design professional familiar with the construction industry. It is recognized, however, that neither the Architect nor the Owner has control over the cost of labor, materials or equipment, over the Contractor's methods of determining bid prices, or over competitive bidding, market or negotiating conditions. Accordingly, the Architect cannot and does not warrant or represent that bids or negotiated prices will not vary from the Project budget proposed, established or approved by the Owner, if any, or from any Statement of Probable Construction Cost or other cost estimate or evaluation prepared by the Architect.

3.2.2 No fixed limit of Construction Cost shall be established as a condition of this Agreement by the furnishing, proposal or establishment of a Project budget under Subparagraph 1.1.2 or Paragraph 2.2 or otherwise, unless such fixed limit has been agreed upon in writing and signed by the parties hereto. If such a fixed limit has been established, the Architect shall be permitted to include contingencies for design, bidding and price escalation, to determine what materials, equipment, component systems and types of construction are to be included in the Contract Documents, to make reasonable adjustments in the scope of the Project and to include in the Contract Documents alternate bids to adjust the Construction Cost to the fixed limit. Any such fixed limit shall be increased in the amount of any increase in the Contract Sum occurring after execution of the Contract for Construction.

3.2.3 If the Bidding or Negotiation Phase has not commenced within three months after the Architect submits the Construction Documents to the Owner, any Project budget or fixed limit of Construction Cost shall be adjusted to reflect any change in the general level of prices in the construction industry between the date of submission of the Construction Documents to the Owner and the date on which proposals are sought.

3.2.4 If a Project budget or fixed limit of Construction Cost (adjusted as provided in Subparagraph 3.2.3) is exceeded by the lowest bona fide bid or negotiated proposal, the Owner shall (1) give written approval of an increase in such fixed limit, (2) authorize rebidding or renegotiating of the Project within a reasonable time, (3) if the Project is abandoned, terminate in accordance with Paragraph 10.2, or (4) cooperate in revising the Project scope and quality as required to reduce the Construction Cost. In the case of (4), provided a fixed limit of Construction Cost has been established as a condition of this Agreement, the Architect, without additional charge, shall modify the Drawings and Specifications as necessary to comply with the fixed limit. The providing of such service shall be the limit of the Architect's responsibility arising from the establishment of such fixed limit, and having done so, the Architect shall be entitled to compensation for all services performed, in accordance with this Agreement, whether or not the Construction Phase is commenced.

ARTICLE 4
DIRECT PERSONNEL EXPENSE

4.1 Direct Personnel Expense is defined as the direct salaries of all the Architect's personnel engaged on the Project, and the portion of the cost of their mandatory and customary contributions and benefits related thereto, such as employment taxes and other statutory employee benefits, insurance, sick leave, holidays, vacations, pensions and similar contributions and benefits.

ARTICLE 5
REIMBURSABLE EXPENSES

5.1 Reimbursable Expenses are in addition to the Compensation for Basic and Additional Services and include actual expenditures made by the Architect and the Architect's employees and consultants in the interest of the Project for the expenses listed in the following Subparagraphs:

5.1.1 Expense of transportation in connection with the Project; living expenses in connection with out-of-town travel; long distance communications, and fees paid for securing approval of authorities having jurisdiction over the Project.

5.1.2 Expense of reproductions, postage and handling of Drawings, Specifications and other documents, excluding reproductions for the office use of the Architect and the Architect's consultants.

5.1.3 Expense of data processing and photographic production techniques when used in connection with Additional Services.

5.1.4 If authorized in advance by the Owner, expense of overtime work requiring higher than regular rates.

5.1.5 Expense of renderings, models and mock-ups requested by the Owner.

5.1.6 Expense of any additional insurance coverage or limits, including professional liability insurance, requested by the Owner in excess of that normally carried by the Architect and the Architect's consultants.

ARTICLE 6
PAYMENTS TO THE ARCHITECT

6.1 PAYMENTS ON ACCOUNT OF BASIC SERVICES

6.1.1 An initial payment as set forth in Paragraph 14.1 is the minimum payment under this Agreement.

6.1.2 Subsequent payments for Basic Services shall be made monthly and shall be in proportion to services performed within each Phase of services, on the basis set forth in Article 14.

6.1.3 If and to the extent that the Contract Time initially established in the Contract for Construction is exceeded or extended through no fault of the Architect, compensation for any Basic Services required for such extended period of Administration of the Construction Contract shall be computed as set forth in Paragraph 14.4 for Additional Services.

6.1.4 When compensation is based on a percentage of Construction Cost, and any portions of the Project are deleted or otherwise not constructed, compensation for such portions of the Project shall be payable to the extent services are performed on such portions, in accordance with the schedule set forth in Subparagraph 14.2.2, based on (1) the lowest bona fide bid or negotiated proposal or, (2) if no such bid or proposal is received, the most recent Statement of Probable Construction Cost or Detailed Estimate of Construction Cost for such portions of the Project.

6.2 PAYMENTS ON ACCOUNT OF ADDITIONAL SERVICES

6.2.1 Payments on account of the Architect's Additional Services as defined in Paragraph 1.7 and for Reimbursable Expenses as defined in Article 5 shall be made monthly upon presentation of the Architect's statement of services rendered or expenses incurred.

6.3 PAYMENTS WITHHELD

6.3.1 No deductions shall be made from the Architect's compensation on account of penalty, liquidated damages or other sums withheld from payments to contractors, or on account of the cost of changes in the Work other than those for which the Architect is held legally liable.

6.4 PROJECT SUSPENSION OR TERMINATION

6.4.1 If the Project is suspended or abandoned in whole or in part for more than three months, the Architect shall be compensated for all services performed prior to receipt of written notice from the Owner of such suspension or abandonment, together with Reimbursable Expenses then due and all Termination Expenses as defined in Paragraph 10.4. If the Project is resumed after being suspended for more than three months, the Architect's compensation shall be equitably adjusted.

ARTICLE 7
ARCHITECT'S ACCOUNTING RECORDS

7.1 Records of Reimbursable Expenses and expenses pertaining to Additional Services and services performed on the basis of a Multiple of Direct Personnel Expense shall be kept on the basis of generally accepted accounting principles and shall be available to the Owner or the Owner's authorized representative at mutually convenient times.

ARTICLE 8
OWNERSHIP AND USE OF DOCUMENTS

8.1 Drawings and Specifications as instruments of service are and shall remain the property of the Architect whether the Project for which they are made is executed or not. The Owner shall be permitted to retain copies, including reproducible copies, of Drawings and Specifications for information and reference in connection with the Owner's use and occupancy of the Project. The Drawings and Specifications shall not be used by the Owner on other projects, for additions to this Project, or for completion of this Project by others provided the Architect is not in default under this Agreement, except by agreement in writing and with appropriate compensation to the Architect.

8.2 Submission or distribution to meet official regulatory requirements or for other purposes in connection with the Project is not to be construed as publication in derogation of the Architect's rights.

ARTICLE 9
ARBITRATION

9.1 All claims, disputes and other matters in question between the parties to this Agreement, arising out of or relating to this Agreement or the breach thereof, shall be decided by arbitration in accordance with the Construction Industry Arbitration Rules of the American Arbitration Association then obtaining unless the parties mutually agree otherwise. No arbitration, arising out of or relating to this Agreement, shall include, by consolidation, joinder or in any other manner, any additional person not a party to this Agreement except by written consent containing a specific reference to this Agreement and signed by the Architect, the Owner, and any other person sought to be joined. Any consent to arbitration involving an additional person or persons shall not constitute consent to arbitration of any dispute not described therein or with any person not named or described therein. This Agreement to arbitrate and any agreement to arbitrate with an additional person or persons duly consented to by the parties to this Agreement shall be specifically enforceable under the prevailing arbitration law.

9.2 Notice of the demand for arbitration shall be filed in writing with the other party to this Agreement and with the American Arbitration Association. The demand shall be made within a reasonable time after the claim, dispute or other matter in question has arisen. In no event shall the demand for arbitration be made after the date when institution of legal or equitable proceedings based on such claim, dispute or other matter in question would be barred by the applicable statute of limitations.

9.3 The award rendered by the arbitrators shall be final, and judgment may be entered upon it in accordance with applicable law in any court having jurisdiction thereof.

ARTICLE 10
TERMINATION OF AGREEMENT

10.1 This Agreement may be terminated by either party upon seven days' written notice should the other party fail substantially to perform in accordance with its terms through no fault of the party initiating the termination.

10.2 This Agreement may be terminated by the Owner upon at least seven days' written notice to the Architect in the event that the Project is permanently abandoned.

10.3 In the event of termination not the fault of the Architect, the Architect shall be compensated for all services performed to termination date, together with Reimbursable Expenses then due and all Termination Expenses as defined in Paragraph 10.4.

10.4 Termination Expenses include expenses directly attributable to termination for which the Architect is not otherwise compensated, plus an amount computed as a percentage of the total Basic and Additional Compensation earned to the time of termination, as follows:

.1 20 percent if termination occurs during the Schematic Design Phase; or

.2 10 percent if termination occurs during the Design Development Phase; or

.3 5 percent if termination occurs during any subsequent phase.

ARTICLE 11
MISCELLANEOUS PROVISIONS

11.1 Unless otherwise specified, this Agreement shall be governed by the law of the principal place of business of the Architect.

11.2 Terms in this Agreement shall have the same meaning as those in AIA Document A201, General Conditions of the Contract for Construction, current as of the date of this Agreement.

11.3 As between the parties to this Agreement: as to all acts or failures to act by either party to this Agreement, any applicable statute of limitations shall commence to run and any alleged cause of action shall be deemed to have accrued in any and all events not later than the relevant Date of Substantial Completion of the Work, and as to any acts or failures to act occurring after the relevant Date of Substantial Completion, not later than the date of issuance of the final Certificate for Payment.

11.4 The Owner and the Architect waive all rights against each other and against the contractors, consultants, agents and employees of the other for damages covered by any property insurance during construction as set forth in the edition of AIA Document A201, General Conditions, current as of the date of this Agreement. The Owner and the Architect each shall require appropriate similar waivers from their contractors, consultants and agents.

ARTICLE 12
SUCCESSORS AND ASSIGNS

12.1 The Owner and the Architect, respectively, bind themselves, their partners, successors, assigns and legal representatives to the other party to this Agreement and to the partners, successors, assigns and legal representatives of such other party with respect to all covenants of this Agreement. Neither the Owner nor the Architect shall assign, sublet or transfer any interest in this Agreement without the written consent of the other.

ARTICLE 13
EXTENT OF AGREEMENT

13.1 This Agreement represents the entire and integrated agreement between the Owner and the Architect and supersedes all prior negotiations, representations or agreements, either written or oral. This Agreement may be amended only by written instrument signed by both Owner and Architect.

ARTICLE 14

BASIS OF COMPENSATION

The Owner shall compensate the Architect for the Scope of Services provided, in accordance with Article 6, Payments to the Architect, and the other Terms and Conditions of this Agreement, as follows:

14.1 AN INITIAL PAYMENT of   dollars ($)

shall be made upon execution of this Agreement and credited to the Owner's account as follows:

14.2 BASIC COMPENSATION

14.2.1 FOR BASIC SERVICES, as described in Paragraphs 1.1 through 1.5, and any other services included in Article 15 as part of Basic Services, Basic Compensation shall be computed as follows:

(Here insert basis of compensation, including fixed amounts, multiples or percentages, and identify Phases to which particular methods of compensation apply, if necessary.)

14.2.2 Where compensation is based on a Stipulated Sum or Percentage of Construction Cost, payments for Basic Services shall be made as provided in Subparagraph 6.1.2, so that Basic Compensation for each Phase shall equal the following percentages of the total Basic Compensation payable:

(Include any additional Phases as appropriate.)

Schematic Design Phase:	percent (%)
Design Development Phase:	percent (%)
Construction Documents Phase:	percent (%)
Bidding or Negotiation Phase:	percent (%)
Construction Phase:	percent (%)

14.3 FOR PROJECT REPRESENTATION BEYOND BASIC SERVICES, as described in Paragraph 1.6, Compensation shall be computed separately in accordance with Subparagraph 1.6.2.

136 APPENDIX 2

14.4 COMPENSATION FOR ADDITIONAL SERVICES

14.4.1 FOR ADDITIONAL SERVICES OF THE ARCHITECT, as described in Paragraph 1.7, and any other services included in Article 15 as part of Additional Services, but excluding Additional Services of consultants, Compensation shall be computed as follows:

(Here insert basis of compensation, including rates and/or multiples of Direct Personnel Expense for Principals and employees, and identify Principals and classify employees, if required. Identify specific services to which particular methods of compensation apply, if necessary.)

14.4.2 FOR ADDITIONAL SERVICES OF CONSULTANTS, including additional structural, mechanical and electrical engineering services and those provided under Subparagraph 1.7.21 or identified in Article 15 as part of Additional Services, a multiple of (   ) times the amounts billed to the Architect for such services.

(Identify specific types of consultants in Article 15, if required.)

14.5 FOR REIMBURSABLE EXPENSES, as described in Article 5, and any other items included in Article 15 as Reimbursable Expenses, a multiple of (   ) times the amounts expended by the Architect, the Architect's employees and consultants in the interest of the Project.

14.6 Payments due the Architect and unpaid under this Agreement shall bear interest from the date payment is due at the rate entered below, or in the absence thereof, at the legal rate prevailing at the principal place of business of the Architect.

(Here insert any rate of interest agreed upon.)

(Usury laws and requirements under the Federal Truth in Lending Act, similar state and local consumer credit laws and other regulations at the Owner's and Architect's principal places of business, the location of the Project and elsewhere may affect the validity of this provision. Specific legal advice should be obtained with respect to deletion, modification, or other requirements such as written disclosures or waivers.)

14.7 The Owner and the Architect agree in accordance with the Terms and Conditions of this Agreement that:

14.7.1 IF THE SCOPE of the Project or of the Architect's Services is changed materially, the amounts of compensation shall be equitably adjusted.

14.7.2 IF THE SERVICES covered by this Agreement have not been completed within

( ) months of the date hereof, through no fault of the Architect, the amounts of compensation, rates and multiples set forth herein shall be equitably adjusted.

ARTICLE 15
OTHER CONDITIONS OR SERVICES

138　APPENDIX 2

This Agreement entered into as of the day and year first written above.

OWNER   ARCHITECT
_____   _____
_____   _____
_____   _____

BY_____   BY_____

12 B141-1977　　**AIA DOCUMENT B141** • OWNER-ARCHITECT AGREEMENT • THIRTEENTH EDITION • JULY 1977 • AIA® • © 1977
　　　　　　　　　　　THE AMERICAN INSTITUTE OF ARCHITECTS, 1735 NEW YORK AVENUE, N.W., WASHINGTON, D.C. 20006

Appendix 3

THE AMERICAN INSTITUTE OF ARCHITECTS

AIA Document A101

Standard Form of Agreement Between Owner and Contractor

where the basis of payment is a
STIPULATED SUM

1977 EDITION

THIS DOCUMENT HAS IMPORTANT LEGAL CONSEQUENCES; CONSULTATION WITH
AN ATTORNEY IS ENCOURAGED WITH RESPECT TO ITS COMPLETION OR MODIFICATION

Use only with the 1976 Edition of AIA Document A201, General Conditions of the Contract for Construction.

This document has been approved and endorsed by The Associated General Contractors of America.

AGREEMENT

made as of the   day of   in the year of Nineteen
Hundred and

BETWEEN the Owner:

and the Contractor:

The Project:

The Architect:

The Owner and the Contractor agree as set forth below.

Copyright 1915, 1918, 1925, 1937, 1951, 1958, 1961, 1963, 1967, 1974, © 1977 by the American Institute of Architects, 1735 New York Avenue, N.W., Washington, D. C. 20006. Reproduction of the material herein or substantial quotation of its provisions without permission of the AIA violates the copyright laws of the United States and will be subject to legal prosecution.

ARTICLE 1
THE CONTRACT DOCUMENTS

The Contract Documents consist of this Agreement, the Conditions of the Contract (General, Supplementary and other Conditions), the Drawings, the Specifications, all Addenda issued prior to and all Modifications issued after execution of this Agreement. These form the Contract, and all are as fully a part of the Contract as if attached to this Agreement or repeated herein. An enumeration of the Contract Documents appears in Article 7.

ARTICLE 2
THE WORK

The Contractor shall perform all the Work required by the Contract Documents for
(Here insert the caption descriptive of the Work as used on other Contract Documents.)

ARTICLE 3
TIME OF COMMENCEMENT AND SUBSTANTIAL COMPLETION

The Work to be performed under this Contract shall be commenced

and, subject to authorized adjustments, Substantial Completion shall be achieved not later than

(Here insert any special provisions for liquidated damages relating to failure to complete on time.)

ARTICLE 4

CONTRACT SUM

The Owner shall pay the Contractor in current funds for the performance of the Work, subject to additions and deductions by Change Order as provided in the Contract Documents, the Contract Sum of

The Contract Sum is determined as follows:
(State here the base bid or other lump sum amount, accepted alternates, and unit prices, as applicable.)

ARTICLE 5

PROGRESS PAYMENTS

Based upon Applications for Payment submitted to the Architect by the Contractor and Certificates for Payment issued by the Architect, the Owner shall make progress payments on account of the Contract Sum to the Contractor as provided in the Contract Documents for the period ending the   day of the month as follows:

Not later than   days following the end of the period covered by the Application for Payment   percent (%) of the portion of the Contract Sum properly allocable to labor, materials and equipment incorporated in the Work and   percent (%) of the portion of the Contract Sum properly allocable to materials and equipment suitably stored at the site or at some other location agreed upon in writing, for the period covered by the Application for Payment, less the aggregate of previous payments made by the Owner; and upon Substantial Completion of the entire Work, a sum sufficient to increase the total payments to   percent (%) of the Contract Sum, less such amounts as the Architect shall determine for all incomplete Work and unsettled claims as provided in the Contract Documents.

(If not covered elsewhere in the Contract Documents, here insert any provision for limiting or reducing the amount retained after the Work reaches a certain stage of completion.)

Payments due and unpaid under the Contract Documents shall bear interest from the date payment is due at the rate entered below, or in the absence thereof, at the legal rate prevailing at the place of the Project.
(Here insert any rate of interest agreed upon.)

Usury laws and requirements under the Federal Truth in Lending Act, similar state and local consumer credit laws and other regulations at the Owner's and Contractor's principal places of business, the location of the Project and elsewhere may affect the validity of this provision. Specific legal advice should be obtained with respect to deletion, modification, or other requirements such as written disclosures or waivers.

ARTICLE 6

FINAL PAYMENT

Final payment, constituting the entire unpaid balance of the Contract Sum, shall be paid by the Owner to the Contractor when the Work has been completed, the Contract fully performed, and a final Certificate for Payment has been issued by the Architect.

ARTICLE 7

MISCELLANEOUS PROVISIONS

7.1 Terms used in this Agreement which are defined in the Conditions of the Contract shall have the meanings designated in those Conditions.

7.2 The Contract Documents, which constitute the entire agreement between the Owner and the Contractor, are listed in Article 1 and, except for Modifications issued after execution of this Agreement, are enumerated as follows:

(List below the Agreement, the Conditions of the Contract (General, Supplementary, and other Conditions), the Drawings, the Specifications, and any Addenda and accepted alternates, showing page or sheet numbers in all cases and dates where applicable.)

This Agreement entered into as of the day and year first written above.

OWNER   CONTRACTOR

_____   _____

BY   BY

_____   _____

AIA DOCUMENT A101 • OWNER-CONTRACTOR AGREEMENT • ELEVENTH EDITION • JUNE 1977 • AIA®
©1977 • THE AMERICAN INSTITUTE OF ARCHITECTS, 1735 NEW YORK AVE., N.W., WASHINGTON, D. C. 20006   A101-1977

Index

Index

Adjacent buildings, 13
Advances, 78, 82
Air conditioning, 66
Appraiser, 77
Arbitration, 58
Architect, 55-70
    agreement with, 58, 125-136
    compensation, 58-60
    duties, 56
    payment, 60
    role, 61-70
    selection, 55
Asking price, 19

Bid, 68, 90, 95
Binder, insurance, 45
Bond
    lien, 83
    performance, 97
    roof, 98
Broker
    as consultant, 17
    mortgage, 77-78
    real estate, 16
Building costs, 94-101
Building inspector, 69-70, 90
Bonus, 79

Certificate of Occupancy, 70, 82
Changes, 88, 90
Charges, carrying, 39
Closing, 22, 48
Codes, building, 64-65
Co-insurance, 42
Commission, 16
Condominium, 23-24, 83
Construction, time, 42
Construction documents, 68
Contract, 50-51
Contractor, 68, 87-93
    agreement with owner, 137-142
    bidding procedure, 90
    choice of, 89
    guarantee, 93
    union and non-union, 68-69
Cooperative, 24-26, 83
Costs
    building, 94-101
    guidelines, 100-101

Deed, 51
Depreciation, 29
Dummy corporation, 83

Elevations, 74
Escrow, 50
Eviction, 39
Expense control, 30, 32

Fees
    brokerage, 16
    lender, 79
FHA, 92
Financing, 53, 77-83
    commitment, 78
    payments, 82
    subordination, 80
Forms
    expense, 33, 35
    rent, 33-34
    reporting, 32

Harassment, 39
    reverse, 39-40
Heating, 66-67

Inspector, building, 69-70, 90
Insurance, 41-46, 120
    agent, 41
    basic coverage, 42
    binders, 3
    broker, 41
    certificates, 45
    co-insurance, 42

Insurance (continued)
   homeowners, 120
   liability, 42
   losses, 45
   personal property, 120
   survey, 44
   title, 48, 79
   workmen's compensation, 44
Interest rates, 79
Interior design, 71-76

Joists, floor, 100

Large scale reconstruction, 4-6
Lawyer
   fees, 48
   financing, 53
   role in acquisition, 48-52
   selection, 47
Layout, 62
Lease, 36, 118
   sublease, 119
Legal aspects, 47-54
Liens, 83
Loan(s)
   construction, 53
   payments, 82
   second mortgage construction, 81
Location, 13-16

Management, 29-35
Mechanical systems, 66-67
Mortgage, 77-79
   broker, 78
   costs, 78
   negotiated direct, 77-78
   second, 80
   second, construction, 81

Negotiating strategy, 19-22
Neighborhood, 13
   analysis, 13-14

Offers, 20
Operating loss, 30
Owner
   agreement with architect, 125-136
   agreement with contractor, 137-142
Ownership method, 52-53

Partnership, 26-28
Pay-off, 92

Penalty, prepayment, 80
Performance bond, 97
Permit, building, 64
Pets, 118
Petty cash, 33
Plans, 62
Points, 54, 79
Postclosing, 52
Punch list, 69, 82
Purchase money mortgage, 50-51

Relocation
   budget, 37
   cost, 36, 39
   tenant, 36
Renovation prior to purchase, 9-12
Rents, 37, 115

Security, 102-111
   alarms, 110
   bars and gates, 102-105
   chains, 109
   cylinders, 108
   door, 105-106
   locks, 107-108
   roof, 106
   safes, 109
   television, 106
   viewers, 109
Specifications, 65-66
Sublease, 119
Subordination, 80-82
Superintendent, 30
   salary, 32

Take-out, 53
Telephone installation, 112-113
Tenant
   relocation, 36
   selection, 116-118
   statutory, 38
Title
   closing, 48
   insurance, 48, 79
   report, 51

Vacant building, 29
Values, real estate, 14
Violations, 52

Working drawings, 65